CRIMINAL
INVESTIGATIONS

TERRORISM

CRIMINAL INVESTIGATIONS

CRIMINAL
INVESTIGATIONS

TERRORISM

BEN MALISOW

CONSULTING EDITOR: **JOHN L. FRENCH**,

CRIME SCENE SUPERVISOR,
BALTIMORE POLICE CRIME LABORATORY

CHELSEA HOUSE
P U B L I S H E R S
An imprint of Infobase Publishing

CRIMINAL INVESTIGATIONS: Terrorism

Chelsea House
An imprint of Infobase Publishing
132 West 31st Street
New York NY 10001

Library of Congress Cataloging-in-Publication Data
Malisow, Ben.
Terrorism / Ben Malisow ; consulting editor John L. French ; crime scene
supervisor Baltimore Police Crime Laboratory. — 1st ed.
p. cm. — (Criminal investigations)
Includes bibliographical references and index.
ISBN-13: 978-0-7910-9412-9 (alk. paper)
ISBN-10: 0-7910-9412-X (alk. paper)
1. Terrorism—Juvenile literature. I. French, John L. II. Title. III. Series.
HV6431.M357 2008   363.325—dc22
2008012306

Chelsea House books are available at special discounts when purchased
in bulk quantities for businesses, associations, institutions,
or sales promotions. Please call our Special Sales Department
in New York at (212) 967-8800 or (800) 322-8755.

You can find Chelsea House on the World Wide Web at
http://www.chelseahouse.com

Text design by Erika K. Arroyo
Cover design by Ben Peterson
Chapter 10 generated by Infobase Publishing.

Cover: Police and investigators look at what remains of the flight deck of
Pan Am 103 on a field in Lockerbie, Scotland, in 1988.

Printed in the United States of America

Bang EJB 10 9 8 7 6 5 4 3 2 1

This book is printed on acid-free paper.

All links and Web addresses were checked and verified to be
correct at the time of publication. Because of the dynamic nature
of the Web, some addresses and links may have changed
since publication and may no longer be valid.

Contents

Foreword

In 2000 there were 15,000 murders in the United States. During that same year about a half million people were assaulted, 1.1 million cars were stolen, 400,000 robberies took place, and more than 2 million homes and businesses were broken into. All told, in the last year of the twentieth century, there were more than 11 million crimes committed in this country.*

In 2000 the population of the United States was approximately 280 million people. If each of the above crimes happened to a separate person, only 4 percent of the country would have been directly affected. Yet everyone is in some way affected by crime. Taxes pay patrolmen, detectives, and scientists to investigate it, lawyers and judges to prosecute it, and correctional officers to watch over those convicted of committing it. Crimes against businesses cause prices to rise as their owners pass on the cost of theft and security measures installed to prevent future losses. Tourism in cities, and the money it brings in, may rise and fall in part due to stories about crime in their streets. And every time someone is shot, stabbed, beaten, or assaulted, or when someone is jailed for having committed such a crime, not only they suffer but so may their friends, family, and loved ones. Crime affects everyone.

It is the job of the police to investigate crime with the purpose of putting the bad guys in jail and keeping them there, hoping thereby to punish past crimes and discourage new ones. To accomplish this a police officer has to be many things: dedicated, brave, smart, honest, and imaginative. Luck helps, but it's not required. And there's one more virtue that should be associated with law enforcement. A good police officer is patient.

Patience is a virtue in crime fighting because police officers and detectives know something that most criminals don't. It's not a secret, but most lawbreakers don't learn it until it is too late. Criminals who make money robbing people, breaking into houses, or stealing cars; who live by dealing drugs or committing murder; who spend their days on the wrong side of the law, or commit any other crimes, must remember this: a criminal has to get away with every crime he or she commits. However, to get criminals off the street and put them behind bars, the police only have to catch a criminal once.

The methods by which police catch criminals are varied. Some are as old as recorded history and others are so new that they have yet to be tested in court. One of the first stories in the Bible is of murder, when Cain killed his brother Abel (Genesis 4:1–16). With few suspects to consider and an omniscient detective, this was an easy crime to solve. However, much later in that same work, a young man named Daniel steps in when a woman is accused of an immoral act by two elders (Daniel 13:1–63). By using the standard police practice of separating the witnesses before questioning them, he is able to arrive at the truth of the matter.

From the time of the Bible to almost present day, police investigations did not progress much further than questioning witnesses and searching the crime scene for obvious clues as to a criminal's identity. It was not until the late 1800s that science began to be employed. In 1879 the French began to use physical measurements and later photography to identify repeat offenders. In the same year a Scottish missionary in Japan used a handprint found on a wall to exonerate a man accused of theft. In 1892 a bloody fingerprint led Argentine police to charge and convict a mother of killing her children, and by 1905 Scotland Yard had convicted several criminals thanks to this new science.

Progress continued. By the 1920s scientists were using blood analysis to determine if recovered stains were from the victim or suspect, and the new field of firearms examination helped link bullets to the guns that fired them.

Nowadays, things are even harder on criminals, when by leaving behind a speck of blood, dropping a sweat-stained hat, or even taking a sip from a can of soda, they can give the police everything they need to identify and arrest them.

In the first decade of the twenty-first century the main tools used by the police include

- questioning witnesses and suspects
- searching the crime scene for physical evidence
- employing informants and undercover agents
- investigating the whereabouts of previous offenders when a crime they've been known to commit has occurred
- using computer databases to match evidence found on one crime scene to that found on others or to previously arrested suspects
- sharing information with other law enforcement agencies via the Internet
- using modern communications to keep the public informed and enlist their aid in ongoing investigations

But just as they have many different tools with which to solve crime, so too do they have many different kinds of crime and criminals to investigate. There is murder, kidnapping, and bank robbery. There are financial crimes committed by con men who gain their victim's trust or computer experts who hack into computers. There are criminals who have formed themselves into gangs and those who are organized into national syndicates. And there are those who would kill as many people as possible, either for the thrill of taking a human life or in the horribly misguided belief that it will advance their cause.

The Criminal Investigations series looks at all of the above and more. Each book in the series takes one type of crime and gives the reader an overview of the history of the crime, the methods and motives behind it, the people who have committed it, and the means by which these people are caught and punished. In this series celebrity crimes will be discussed and exposed. Mysteries that have yet to be solved will be presented. Readers will discover the truth about murderers, serial killers, and bank robbers whose stories have become myths and legends. These books will explain how criminals can separate a person from his hard-earned cash, how they prey on the weak and helpless, what is being done to stop them, and what one can do to help prevent becoming a victim.

John L. French,
Crime Scene Supervisor,
Baltimore Police Crime Laboratory

* Federal Bureau of Investigation. "Uniform Crime Reports, Crime in the United States 2000." Available online. URL: http://www.fbi.gov/ucr/00cius.htm. Accessed January 11, 2008.

Acknowledgments

Very special thanks to Art and all the other nice folks in the Las Vegas Public Library system; they are as understanding and patient as they are gracious.

More thanks to Sophia and the rest of the wonderful staff at the UNLV Lied Library, especially in light of my egregious breach of library decorum.

Jerry DeMaio, a good friend to have.

Bob Anderson, spokesperson at the United States Postal Service.

Craig Malisow, whose Web-research skills are far superior to mine.

Introduction:
What is Terrorism?

Since the attacks on the World Trade Center and the Pentagon and the loss of Flight 93 on September 11, 2001, most people have become more concerned with terrorism and possible terrorist activity. Unfortunately, most people don't really know a lot about terrorism, what it really is, and what it is used for.

This book, in addition to offering some insight into and examples of terrorism, will try to answer those questions.

To start, here is some important information.

- Killing someone is not terrorism; it is called murder.
- Killing someone famous is not terrorism; it is called assassination.
- Killing lots of people is not terrorism; it is called mass murder.
- Scaring someone with potential violence is not terrorism; it is called assault.
- Hurting someone is not terrorism; it is called battery.
- Wrecking something is not terrorism; it is called destruction of property.
- Taking something from someone secretly is not terrorism; it is called theft.
- Taking something from someone with force is not terrorism; it is called robbery.
- Forcing someone into a sexual act is not terrorism; it is called rape.

- Threatening harm to get something is not terrorism; it is called extortion.
- Taking hidden information is not terrorism; it is called espionage.

Yet all of these, and many other crimes, can be used by terrorists to conduct terrorist activity. Terrorism is not limited to a certain type of behavior or a particular method.

What is terrorism, then?

Terrorism is scaring someone into doing something they wouldn't do otherwise. For example, a bully in school might want to get a friend elected to the student government. To do this, the bully might threaten to beat up anyone who didn't vote for the bully's friend. The bully is using terrorist tactics (a "tactic" is a method or technique): the bully is scaring the victims into doing something (voting for the bully's friend) that the victims might not do unless the victims were scared. If the bully weren't scaring the victims, they would vote for whomever they wanted.

But what if some of the bully's victims start to think that maybe the bully won't really hurt them, that the bully is just making threats, and won't ever really harm any of the victims? If the victims think they aren't going to be hurt after all, they might decide to ignore the bully. The bully might realize this. The bully has to make a choice, then, too. Either the bully has to live with the fact that there will be fewer votes for the bully's friend, or the bully has to choose to act: the bully has to demonstrate that the threat is very real, that pain and harm will come to those who refuse to do what the bully wants.

The bully has to hurt someone. One of the victims must be attacked, as an example to the rest of them. Once the victims see that the bully is really willing to hurt them, they might consider voting for the bully's friend.

Of course, voting is done in secret—both the bully and the other students know this. No matter how many threats the bully makes, the students know they can vote for whomever they want on election day. The bully knows this, too.

So the bully might try to increase pressure on the rest of the students by making more attacks: the bully might attack another student, and another...one per day, right up until election day. And the bully could threaten everyone that if the bully's friend isn't elected, the bully will attack one person each day, every day after the election. The students might become very frightened of the bully and really believe the bully's threats. The students might consider voting for the bully's friend, just to try to do their part to stop the bully from hurting them, eventually.

That's what terrorism is all about; that's what terrorism is.

Terrorists want to make people do something. In modern terms, terrorism is used for political goals. *Politics* is a word for the way people interact with each other as groups. This is slightly different than the way people interact with each other as individuals; when people interact with each other on a personal level, it is called a relationship. One has a relationship with one's parents, with one's siblings, with one's friends. One decides how one is going to behave in those relationships, whether one is going to enjoy the relationships or hate them, whether or not one trusts the people one has a relationship with, or how to talk to them, what to give them, etc.

Politics, though, is not about individuals; it's about groups —groups of people interacting with each other or with other groups. Today, most political choices, decisions, and activities are controlled by governments—especially governments of nations. Terrorists want to affect those governments and change the way a nation acts by scaring the people in that country.

So how do terrorists scare an entire country full of people into doing something the terrorists want?

First, the terrorists must have a political goal. Acts of violence that are not used to achieve any particular goal are purposeless, and therefore not terrorism. Someone who uses violence or force for no reason is a different kind of bully, one who bullies victims for pleasure. Such a bully may suffer from some emotional or psychological problem.

In our example, the bully wants to achieve a political goal: the bully wants to convince all students to vote for the bully's friend so that person will win the election.

Next, the terrorists must find a way to achieve their political goal using force. If a group of people want to change the way an entire country thinks or feels, but doesn't use force, then those people are not terrorists.

There are many ways to achieve political goals without force. For instance, a group of people could take part in legal political activity, such as trying to get their own candidates elected, or using petitions and postcards to communicate their feelings to politicians, or using mass media to communicate their message to the rest of a country's citizens. Or they could take part in peaceful protests and demonstrations. Finally, they might even do something that's illegal but doesn't usually harm anyone else, such as civil disobedience or passive resistance.

If someone uses any of these nonviolent tactics, they are not terrorists. Terrorists have to use force and have to hurt someone or threaten to hurt someone in order to be terrorists.

In our example, the bully uses force: the bully actually beats students, harming them physically.

Finally, terrorists use their victims as examples. By hurting or killing someone, the terrorists send a message to everyone else: "Do what we want you to do, or we might hurt or kill *you* next time." If everyone else believes the terrorists, then the country might change to meet the terrorists' demands. The terrorists might achieve their goals through the use of force.

ϙ ORIGINS OF THE WORD *TERRORIST*

After the American Revolution, the people of France decided to follow suit and have their own rebellion. Once the government was overthrown, the rebels still had a problem: different groups within the country wanted different things.

Some groups wanted to make a lot of new changes. Some groups didn't think the revolution went far enough, and wanted to engage in more killing and warfare. And some groups wanted to make France go back to the way it was.

That last group was mostly made up of the rich people and the royalty, who had lost a great deal of power and wealth during the revolution.

Another group, named the Jacobins, wanted to make sure that the changes created by the revolution did not disappear. Therefore, in September of 1793, they began the Reign of Terror.

The Reign of Terror was a way to ensure that people inside of France followed the new government's rules. Anyone who didn't follow the rules, or who caused trouble, could be arrested, beaten,

Sometimes, after a terrorist attack, people who weren't victims don't believe the terrorists. People who weren't hurt or killed don't believe that the terrorists can hurt them individually. In that case, they ignore the terrorists' demands, and don't change anything. When that happens, the terrorists have not achieved their political goals and must decide whether to give up or to try again.

The terrorists might decide that achieving their goals is impossible because people aren't getting scared. If the terrorists are trying to frighten people (terrorizing them), and people aren't getting frightened, then the terrorists are failing.

The terrorists might decide, on the other hand, that more attacks are necessary, that if more people are hurt or killed, then the rest of the people will eventually become afraid. The terrorists might continue their efforts to achieve their goals through force.

In our example, the bully can't beat up every student at once, but the bully can beat up one or two every day. And if this happens, all the students might believe that they will eventually be beaten

and murdered. And any French citizen had the right to take part in this "war." Any French person could report another citizen to the police, or arrest someone, or even attack them. During this time, everyone was authorized to be a vigilante.

The Jacobins were at the front of the Reign of Terror. They accused people of being enemies against France, arrested many, beat some to death, and dragged many, many more to the guillotine. Supposedly, the Jacobins called themselves "terrorists," and were proud of it. Their leader, Robespierre, put it like this: "Terror is nothing other than prompt, severe, inflexible justice."

By arresting, beating, and executing some people, the Jacobins hoped to scare everyone else into doing whatever the government wanted.

The Reign of Terror only lasted for about 10 months, but tens of thousands of people were murdered during this time. The Jacobins were eventually banned following a change of power and Robespierre's execution in 1794.

if they don't comply with the bully's demands, even if they haven't been beaten already.

This book will discuss different examples, throughout recent history, of terrorists who tried to accomplish political goals. Some of them were successful; others were not. The book will also explain different types of terrorist attacks, and how the methods are pretty much the same (hurting and killing people), but the goals are very different.

The book will also cover a very important facet of terrorism: how to deal with terrorism, both after a terrorist attack has occurred and before it happens, to try to prevent it. As in our example, the more activity the terrorist conducts, the more likely that the terrorist will be caught and punished. If our bully increases attacks to one per day, it's quite likely that the bully will be caught, for a number of reasons: there are more chances the bully will be seen in the act by a teacher or administrator; as the number of victims rises, parents and others might become aware of a large problem at the school; as the danger to each student increases, they may *all* become more desperate, and consider ganging up on the bully. Where they once feared the bully, they may become more afraid of not fighting back.

There is one important thing to remember. This book will use the following definition for terrorism:

> An illegal use of force against a small number of victims to accomplish political goals by persuading a large number of people to change political policies or ideas.

Republican Terrorism

On September 11, 1867, two men were arrested in Manchester, England. They were Colonel Timothy J. Kelly, an American who fought for the Union in the Civil War, and Captain Timothy Deasey, from County Cork, in Ireland.

They were also members of the Irish Republican Brotherhood (IRB), also known as the Fenians. The IRB was a group bent on ending British control of Ireland and freeing Ireland to be its own nation.

The police knew that the men worked for the IRB, and were fairly certain that they were in Manchester to plan the bombing of several government buildings there. But there was no proof, at least none they could obtain without revealing certain spies and informers within the IRB ranks. So Kelly and Deasey were held on a charge of vagrancy, or basically, being homeless.

On September 18, the police were in the process of moving the prisoners from a courthouse to another location. The police had already been warned that the IRB intended to try to "rescue" Kelly and Deasey—to break them out of prison.[1] Extra guards had been posted—12 in all, on horseback. Kelly and Deasey were locked in the back of an enclosed, horsedrawn police wagon, guarded by a police sergeant.

Partway through the journey, 30 IRB terrorists surrounded the wagon, forcing it to halt. They shot one of the horses pulling the wagon so it could not take off. The IRB men had guns, but the police didn't, so the police had to retreat, leaving the wagon unguarded, except for one man, Police Sergeant Brett, locked in the back of the wagon with the prisoners.

The IRB men yelled at Brett to unlock the wagon; Brett refused. One of the IRB men fired a shot: Brett was hit. Another prisoner inside the wagon took the keys from Brett and gave them to Kelly and Deasey. The IRB prisoners unlocked themselves from the wagon and fled with their rescuers.

Police Sergeant Brett was dead.

British King Henry II sent troops into Ireland in 1156, and they pretty much never left.[2] Historians argue over the reason why the British first invaded Ireland, but England remained involved over the centuries because Ireland is right next-door, and the English always had a political, religious, or security excuse for not leaving. Over the years, different Irish groups had risen, trying to get rid of the British, mostly without much success. This group, the IRB, formed in 1858,[3] became a major force in rebellion and the use of terror tactics.

The killing of Police Sergeant Brett was the result of terrorism, because the IRB attack on the police van was terrorism. Attacking the van was an illegal (criminal) use of force (armed attackers against police) against a small number of victims (the cops guarding the van) to accomplish political goals ("freeing" Ireland) by persuading a large number of people (the Irish and British populaces) to change political policies (Britain out of Ireland) or ideas (that the Brits controlled Ireland, and that the rebels couldn't operate with impunity against a larger, better-equipped, better-armed, better-financed foe).

The daring and violent rescue raid had been a small-scale success for the IRB: the immediate goal, rescuing the captives, was accomplished. But there were many unforeseen results; some worked in favor of the rebels, and some in favor of the British government.

The first thing that happened, right after the rescue operation, was that the police regrouped and went out looking for the perpetrators. Many men were captured quickly, on the same day as the attack. Some say that most of these men were innocent, and that the police grabbed them because they knew these men as IRB sympathizers or collaborators, whether or not they took part in the rescue operation.

Five men eventually stood trial for the crimes related to the rescue. The government wanted a fast, brutal response, because they wanted to show any terrorists, or potential terrorists, that terrorism was not acceptable behavior and that killing a policeman would result in the worst punishments.

On November 23, 1867, three men were hanged for the crime. The government had tried using the tactics of shock and fear: by demonstrating its willingness to kill terrorists, the government hoped to convince others not to carry out similar activities.

Unfortunately, that was probably not the best tactic; as many other governments, dealing with many other terrorists, would eventually learn, killing people is sometimes not an effective way of stomping out terrorism. In this particular case, killing the three IRB men for the murder of Police Sergeant Brett actually worked against the government.

Even before the trial, the IRB started a public relations campaign to convince people—both Irish and English—that the men on trial were not involved in the terrorist operation, and, even if they were, they had not fired the shot that killed Police Sergeant Brett. At the trial, the three men started yelling a battle cry ("God save Ireland!") for a free Ireland, a battle cry that was picked up and used by other IRB terrorists, and those that came after them, for many, many years. After the execution, the dead men were not known as "Brett's killers"; they became known, to many Irish people and revolutionaries in particular, as the "Manchester Martyrs."

A martyr is someone who dies for a cause; usually, the term implies that they were wrongly accused or unjustly punished.

Whether or not the men were terrorists, whether or not they took part in the operation, and whether or not they were directly responsible for Brett's death (and whether or not that death was intentional) eventually became unimportant. The truth soon didn't matter. Managing the story was much more important.

By dictating what people would believe, the rebels took away the power from the government. The government wanted one thing—swift, harsh justice—and ended up with another: the appearance that the government had killed three brave, possibly innocent men. Even today, historians disagree as to whether the men who were executed had committed the crimes of which they were accused.

Of course, the trial and executions were not the only tools the British government tried to use after the rescue operation.

For instance, the British had been using, and continued to use, an extensive network of spies and informants. Spies are employees who go undercover and pretend to be something they are not in order to get information or to cause trouble for the group they pretend to join. Informants are members of organizations that are

James Stephens, founder of the Irish Republican Brotherhood. *Sean Sexton Collection/Corbis*

willing to sell inside information. The British government used both against the IRB and similar groups, with some success and some failure.

The British government also created a new law enforcement entity, specially equipped and tasked to deal with the threat of Irish revolutionary terrorists. This organization was called the Special Irish Branch, and it was chartered in March 1883.[4] This group would develop and practice many counterterror tactics long before any other law enforcement entity in the world. Eventually, the organization was renamed "Special Branch," and it still performs many activities in the effort to mitigate the threat of terrorism. In the early 1990s, approximately $50 million was invested in massive British crime surveillance and reporting networks, with significant hopes that these systems could be used against Irish terrorists. Many government functions, from traffic cameras to border checkpoints to driver's license offices, were linked together in England in recent years, allowing police and military personnel to track the movements and behavior of almost any citizen.

The IRB would change, morph, and grow, too. The man who many call the founder of the IRB, James Stephens, died in 1901.[5] The IRB itself disbanded in 1921, as part of a treaty between Ireland and England.[6] But the notion of an Ireland without any British in it, and the tactics to create such a place, remained for a long, long time. Eventually, a new group replaced the IRB; it was called the IRA, the Irish Republican Army, and it hosted some of the most violent, brutal terrorists the world has ever known. Sinn Fein, a group of Irish nationalists who even the IRA thought were too extreme, would pick up the Fenian cause.

The more modern groups often used the battle cry initiated by the IRB Manchester Martyrs.

LESSONS LEARNED

The IRB was interested in creating a nation. They used terror tactics to accomplish this, with a very specific goal in mind: by causing enough trouble and gaining enough attention, the IRB hoped to convince civilians, especially the citizens of Ireland and Great Britain, that the British government should leave Ireland. Other terrorist groups would use the example set by the IRB many times again.

Perhaps more importantly, other governments, when faced with terrorists, were able to better understand how to deal with—and fight—terrorism. The following sections explore some of the things that both groups, terrorists and governments, learned from the experience of the British and the IRB.

Government

■ Unarmed law enforcement personnel are at a distinct disadvantage when faced with a group of armed terrorists.

♀ THE IRISH "TROUBLES"

The fight for Irish independence did not halt with the end of the IRB. Several groups followed, either as offshoots of the original group or just its philosophical heirs. These included:

■ *The Irish Republican Army (IRA)*. Michael Collins, a former president of the IRB, was one of the founders of this group, in the early 1920s. For the rest of the century, different groups would call themselves "the IRA," but few were recognized in the same way as the "Old IRA." Two subgroups formed from an IRA split in 1969: the Provisional IRA and the Official IRA.

■ *The Provisional Irish Republican Army (PIRA)*. An armed group that believed in overthrowing both the British occupation and the Irish Republic, in order to form a unified Ireland. They believed in regulating distinct Irish religious divisions.

■ *The Official Irish Republican Army*. A communist group that wanted to unify all of Ireland, regardless of religious affiliation.

■ *Sinn Fein*. A political party, formed in 1905, dedicated to Irish independence. Like the IRA, many different groups, with many different leaders and goals, have used the name over the past 100 years. At least one such group still exists in Ireland today, as a major political party.

■ *Irish National Liberation Army*. A small, armed group, formed in 1974.

■ Swift, brutal justice is sometimes not the best tactic for long-term success.

Terrorists

■ Manipulating the truth can be even more effective than battle-field success and can cover a significant failure.
■ Future terrorists, and potential terrorists, can be motivated and inspired by the actions of terrorists, even if those original terrorists fail or are punished.

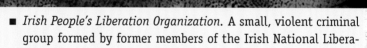

■ *Irish People's Liberation Organization.* A small, violent criminal group formed by former members of the Irish National Liberation Army. This existed from 1986 until 1992.
■ *Real Irish Republican Army (RIRA).* Formed in 1998, by former members of the PIRA, to protest that group's agreement to a peace treaty with Britain.

Irish revolutionary Michael Collins was one of the founders of the Irish Republican Army. *Hulton-Deutsch Collection/Corbis*

COUNTERTERROR TACTICS

Many of the following effective methods are still used today. Governments that know better avoid the ineffective methods, which can be worse than useless; they can harm the government's cause.

Effective

- Find the sources of money and stop them. The British cooperated with American authorities and American groups sympathetic to the Irish cause, and were somewhat effective in cutting off funds for the terrorists.
- If law enforcement moves very soon (a matter of minutes or hours) after an attack, it is likely that some of the participants can be arrested.
- Knowing who the participants might be, before they engage in actual terrorist activity, can be very helpful in capturing terrorists after they've made an attack. The British were very good at creating and maintaining intelligence sources that could give lists of names, addresses, and associates of potential terrorists, and members of groups that had terrorist sympathies and tendencies. By going through these lists, capturing many of those who were involved in the ambush was much easier than if the British had to start from scratch.
- Having a core group of law enforcement personnel who only do counterterror missions is very useful; when police have to do regular community police work, they are less effective in dealing with terrorists because they don't have the extra time, money, effort, and energy. When the British created the Special Branch, it allowed some police personnel to concentrate on just preventing terrorism and catching terrorists, which made law enforcement efforts much more effective.

Ineffective

- Using capital punishment as a message to the terrorists can backfire. The British wanted to cut down on terrorism by showing that terrorists would be executed. Instead, the deaths of the "Manchester Martyrs" only motivated the IRB to continue their campaign of terror, and helped to recruit more IRB members.

The entire "Manchester Martyrs" notion stayed with the Irish for a long time, and was used by other terrorist groups long after the IRB had disbanded.

Utopian Terrorism

Sophia Perovskaya waited for the train to come. She'd been waiting for weeks. And the explosives were finally ready.

Perovskaya was nervous. She and her co-conspirators were going to blow up the train of Czar Alexander II, the ruler of Russia. Weeks before, they had rented a house next to the train tracks, and she had posed as the wife of Lev Gartman, another member of the revolutionary group Narodnaya Volya ("The People's Will" or "The People's Freedom"; the Russian word is flexible).

She remembered hearing the bells in a nearby Moscow church; nine o'clock had come and gone, and the Czar's train wasn't expected until some time between 10 and 11. She fidgeted and waited.

She remembered that they were almost caught twice, and only her hasty action and pure luck had saved them.

While the other rebels dug a tunnel under the tracks, nobody could be allowed in the house; it was Perovskaya's job to keep the operation secret. The first time, they were almost compromised by a private mortgage banker who had come by to inspect the house. While her friends were still digging just a few yards away, Perovskaya stood in the middle of the doorway, arms crossed, and kept repeating that she knew nothing about any mortgage, and that her husband was not at home. Her impersonation of a stupid and stubborn housewife finally made the banker give up and leave.[1]

The second time was even more frightening: a house nearby caught fire. Russian houses were made of wood, and fires spread quickly from house to house. As all the neighbors in the street gathered to help each other evacuate, Perovskaya made other preparations; she placed a bottle of nitroglycerine within range of her pistol. If any police came to search the house, she would shoot the bottle, and blow herself up with as many of authorities as she could.

A half-length portrait of the Russian emperor Alexander II. Alexander ascended the throne in 1855; his rule ended in 1881 when he was assassinated by a member of Narodnaya Volya, a revolutionary group. *Michael Nicholson/Corbis*

When her neighbors pounded on the front door, offering to help Perovskaya carry her belongings out of the house in case it burned, she came to the door carrying a religious icon in upraised arms. She screamed at the people that God would decide whether or not her house and belongings burned, and that they should not try to help her. Her neighbors, very superstitious people, agreed and left.[2]

All that wariness and careful planning had paid off: they were finally ready, and tonight was the night.

Only Perovskaya and a man named Shyrayev remained in the house: all the other rebels, who had helped dig the tunnel and plant the explosives, had fled to a safe distance. Perovskaya knew that there was a good chance she and her partner would be killed in the explosion; the rebel group had experienced problems using the explosives, which were fairly new technology.

She waited. It would not be too long before the train arrived...

There was a sound.

She glanced at her partner. The train was very early. This was strange. Usually, if there was a difference between the scheduled time and the actual time a train ran, then the train was late. It was very rarely early.

Could this be the one?

She discussed it with Shyrayev. They looked for a signal from some of their compatriots, who were stationed a good ways up the track, but saw none.

This must be the train.

Usually, when the czar traveled, he moved with three trains: the first carried his advance team of bodyguards and servants who would prepare each new location for the czar's arrival. The second train contained the plush private carriages of the czar himself. And the third carried the rest of the czar's group.

Perovskaya and her partner made a decision: they would fire the explosives as the next train passed.

They didn't have to wait long. The second train came, and the lookouts gave the signal.

Perovskaya and her fellow terrorist detonated the explosives. The world rocked with the concussion. The noise and fury of a train destroyed in a massive blast was something they could feel for themselves.

Then they fled into the night.

There is disagreement over the results of the explosion that shook the second train in the czar's procession that night. Some say that there were no casualties from the terrorist attack.[3] Some say that many were killed.[4] Sources on the subject even disagree as to whether the attack took place on November 18 or 19, 1879.

But all the sources agree on one important point: the Narodnaya terrorists missed their target.

For some reason, the czar was riding on the first train in the procession, not the second, so the blast missed him completely. Eight train cars were derailed, causing much damage, but it was a train full of servants and luggage.

♀ COUNTERING TERROR

As organizations like the Narodnaya increase their ability to get specialized equipment like sophisticated explosives, governments learn that they have to adapt to these new threats. Over the years, many countries have created their own counterterror units. Most of these are smaller groups drawn from or a part of military and law enforcement special forces. The following is a partial list of some of these groups that are known to the public.

GREAT BRITAIN
- Special Air Service (SAS)
- Special Boat Service (SBS)
- Special Reconnaissance Regiment (SRS)
- Special Branch

UNITED STATES
- 1st Special Forces Operational Detachment-Delta (1st SFOD-D; also called Delta Force)
- Naval Special Warfare Development Group (DEVGRU; formerly known as Seal Team Six)
- Hostage Rescue Team

FRANCE
- National Gendarmes Intervention Group (GIGN)

GERMANY
- GSG 9 der Bundespolizei (GSG9)
- Special Forces Command (KSK)

Even though the czar was not killed or injured, this event turned out to be a big deal. The very fact that someone came so close to blowing him up, and right near Moscow, the capital, too, caused a lot of commotion for both the czar and the people.

This was the actual intent of the Narodnaya group: to cause enough agitation among the government and the common people

AUSTRALIA
- Special Air Service Regiment (SASR)

NEW ZEALAND
- New Zealand Special Air Service (NZ SAS)

ISRAEL
- Sayeret Matkal

CANADA
- Joint Task Force 2 (JTF2)

An Australian Special Air Service Regiment (SASR) trooper scales a ladder in a training exercise. *Darren Hilder/AP*

so that there would be change. The Narodnaya wanted freedom of speech and the press, a constitution, and permanent representation of the people within the government. They figured that this was only possible if the government was scared into making the changes, and that the only way to scare the government was to get all the common people involved.

"Going to the people" was the phrase first used to gather young Russian city dwellers and intellectuals for helping the rural people during a famine. It evolved into a motto that was used to justify all sorts of political activity, including terrorist attacks.

The Narodnaya believed that if they could cause enough damage to the harsh government, all the common people would see that the government could be harmed and would then rise up to join in the revolution.

So, when considering the attack on the czar's train now (128 years later), it could be described as a failure, a success, and a failure.

First, the attack failed because it did not hit the intended target: the czar. More importantly, the people that were hit in the blast, the servants, were exactly the kind of people that the Narodnaya didn't want to hurt. Supposedly, the Narodnaya wanted only to help the common people, which definitely included servants.

Second, the attack was a success because the Narodnaya accomplished one important aspect of their political goal: they got their message "to the people." The use of explosives is always dramatic, but this instance was exceptional. New technology allowed some untrained civilians to cause a massive explosion and actually strike at the government. This was a fairly new and uncommon concept. It got quite a bit of attention in the media, including internationally.

This attack was one in a series of instances where the Narodnaya used explosives to attack the czar. The string of attacks gathered so much attention and caused so much commotion that one historian, Benedict Anderson, wrote that, "Nobel's invention had now arrived politically." Anderson was referring to dynamite, which Alfred Nobel invented in 1866 as a way of stabilizing nitroglycerine.

Another way the attack may be viewed as a success was how it made the government react. By forcing the government to take part in counterterrorist activity, the Narodnaya moved a bit closer to achieving their goals. The Narodnaya believed in "going to the people," and that the people would only react if pushed from both sides: if the government bothered them so much that they ended up hating the government, and if the rebels pushed them into attacking the government.

The government was already troubling the people before the attack. The czar had taken some drastic steps just a few years before to counter what he thought were antigovernment revolutionaries. He started using antiterrorist tactics among a lot of groups that weren't necessarily terrorists. The czar ordered his secret police to investigate groups that printed pamphlets and newsletters that suggested massive governmental changes; he ordered his forces to seize printing presses and arrest writers.

The czar also appointed six military rulers, one for each of Russia's regions, and gave them strict orders to use force in countering rebellious activity. The military rulers were given incredible police powers, and exercised these powers brutally: in several instances, university students were attacked and whipped by armed military personnel on horseback.[5]

Finally, the attacks were a failure in that the Narodnaya's ultimate goal was not achieved. The czar was eventually murdered: on March 1, 1881, Narodnaya terrorists throwing bombs killed him in the street (Perovskaya took part in this attack). But the real goal of the terrorists, the political goal, was to incite rebellion among the common people. That never occurred; the people viewed the entire series of activities—all the attacks on the czar, and the arrests and executions of rebels—as a sort of contest between the government and the rebels. The people didn't want to get involved.

In fact, the people may have been just as afraid, if not more afraid, of the rebels, than they were of the government. Many people were willing to live and work under difficult conditions, conditions that would be considered horrible today, as long as nobody asked them to die for anything or tried to kill them.

The Narodnaya had set out to accomplish a political ideal: they wanted to form a perfect country, with very little government, if any at all. They hoped to make their own country better for everyone, except the government they hated. They failed.

Perovskaya was arrested and hanged a month after she helped kill the czar.

LESSONS LEARNED

The Narodnaya tried to get citizens involved with a revolution, even to take part in terrorist activity. The government and the Narodnaya both learned that the regular people really don't want to get involved; future governments and terrorists may have learned a lot from this example.

Government

- A small group of angry people armed with the latest military technology can hurt or kill just about anyone, including the head of a country.
- Sometimes, police action meant to stop terrorists can, instead, help terrorists by angering more people.
- When terrorists target someone, keeping that person moving and secure is very important. On the day he was assassinated, the czar survived the first bomb thrown at him; he stopped his armored carriage to get out and see if anyone was hurt. The second bomb killed him.

Terrorists

- The media is a very important tool for achieving political goals, but it is very difficult to control. If terrorists use too much force, or make their political message unclear, the media might make the terrorists look too scary, and frighten people they wish to inspire. Modern terrorists realize that managing the media response to an attack is almost as important, if not more so, than planning and carrying out the attack. With more, faster, and better quality media outlets available, media response has become the most important element of terrorism, as with all other political activity.
- Sophisticated ideas might make sense to a small group of people who all believe the same thing, but that doesn't mean the public will agree.
- Getting the people to act, especially to risk their own lives, is extremely difficult.

COUNTERTERROR TACTICS

The methods the czar and his government used to combat terrorism can teach current governments what measures might be successful and which might fail.

Effective

- Using paid informants to find terrorist cells and hiding places can help fight terrorism.
- Acting on tips from the public, especially "strange" circumstances, can lead to important discoveries. The Narodnaya might have been defeated earlier if police had responded to reports of weird smells in certain buildings, where the terrorists were making explosives, or loud industrial sounds in other buildings, where the terrorists ran their printing presses.
- Interrogating captured terrorists can turn up useful information. One Narodnaya agent, Rysakov, quickly broke down after his arrest and gave the police the names and locations of many other terrorists.

Ineffective

- Using military forces against non-terrorist political activists can result in more support for the terrorists and their cause.
- Taking away rights and privileges of the common people may work for a little while, but, if used for too long, can anger more people and drive them to support the terrorists.

Terrorism for Attrition

Foreign troops stationed in a country far from their home need a place to relax. It needs to be safe, and they need to feel secure enough to let down their guard and just enjoy themselves for a little while.

For the British military personnel stationed in occupied Palestine in 1947, that place was the Jerusalem Officers' Club.

After a long week of working in the desert sun and facing hostile forces on all sides of the argument about whether Palestine should belong to the Jews or the Muslims, British military personnel gathered at the Officers' Club on weekends to have some drinks, talk and laugh with each other, commiserate about being away from England, and generally have as good a time as they could. Earlier that year, the club, the building it was in, and at least one other building were cordoned off from the public as part of a British effort to create "security zones" in three large cities within occupied Palestine. All British personnel were to remain in the security zones, where they could be protected, unless they were on duty, and had to be outside. That minimized the danger to British personnel. So, on weekends, the British Officers' Club was supposed to be a good, safe place for the British forces to relax.

The Irgun, a Zionist terrorist group, decided that was a good time for them to strike.

It was March 1, a Saturday afternoon—a day of religious observation for the Jews, but not for the British, which was another reason the military people thought they'd be safe in the club.

A group of Irgun terrorists, more than a dozen in all, met at a nearby girls' school, where they were given instructions, weaponry, and British military uniforms to wear as camouflage.[1]

Two motor vehicles, containing eight terrorists, left the school and drove to the Officers' Club. The vehicles circled the block three times, waiting for the road to be clear of British trucks. Finally, two terrorist strike teams got out of the vehicles and set up defensive positions on the street to cut off any British reinforcements that might arrive after the attack. One set up near a synagogue, the other across the street from the club.

One of the vehicles, a van, sped up and crashed through a barbed-wire fence protecting the British military compound. The van rushed toward the entrance of the facility, where it stopped. When British guards came over to the van to find out if the vehicle had permission to enter the compound, the terrorists mowed them down with automatic weapons-fire.

Three terrorists ran inside the building, each carrying about 100 pounds of explosives, which they placed around pillars that supported the building. As the three terrorists fled, one turned back to get his pistol, which he'd left behind with the explosives. One of the other terrorists grabbed him and they ran out together.

All the terrorists retreated toward the synagogue, then ran past it, to the courtyard of a monastery behind it, where one of the other teams had already cut the fence so they could all get in. In the courtyard, the attack teams gave their weapons and disguises to a group of young, female members of the terrorist group, who put the items in bags; the girls were in charge of escaping with the gear and hiding it.

Soon after the bombers fled, the explosives went off, blowing out the pillars and bringing most of the building to the ground. Inside the Officers' Club, many military personnel were trapped and killed by the explosion and debris. According to one source, British newspapers stated that 20 British military personnel, including three female secretaries, were killed in the attack, and another 30 were wounded.[2]

All the terrorists escaped.

The terrorists were part of a group called the National Military Organization (or "Irgun Zvai Le'umi" in Hebrew), often referred to as just "the Irgun." The Irgun were like many Jews during the first

The British Army Officers' Club in Jerusalem was destroyed by a bomb blast on March 1, 1947, during a wave of terrorist attacks against the British in Palestine that day. *Tom Fitzsimmons/AP*

half of the twentieth century: they wanted a homeland in the Middle East, where the Jews had historically owned a piece of land they called "Israel," off and on for 5,000 years. The people who wanted to create this new version of the old Israel were called "Zionists."

At the time, the British controlled the landmass; they called it "Palestine," or "occupied Palestine," since they were occupying it with military forces and an administrative government. The British faced demands from many different groups of people, including Zionists, native Palestinians, Arabs, and others who wanted to lay permanent claim to what had basically become a British colony.

There were many different types of Zionists, too. Some were peaceful, and merely wanted to settle in the region, coexisting with the people—mostly Palestinians and Arabs—already living there. Others wanted to fight for the land, to take it from the British and the Palestinians. Some were even more brutal than the Irgun; one group, the Stern Gang (sometimes called Lehi), was formed by people who left the Irgun because they thought the Irgun wasn't harsh enough.

Like the Irish Republican Brotherhood (IRB) (see Chapter 1), the militant Zionists wanted to drive out the British and take over the country. The Zionists, however, were going to use a different long-term strategy to achieve their goals because they had an advantage that the Irish didn't: distance. Ireland is right next to Great Britain, so it wasn't much trouble for the British to move military forces there, when necessary. Occupied Palestine, however, is about 2,000 miles from England, so any British military forces stationed in Palestine cost the British government a lot of time, trouble, and money. Winston Churchill, the former Prime Minister of England, said this, in 1946: "One hundred thousand Englishmen are being kept away from their homes and work for a senseless squalid war with the Jews. We are getting ourselves hated and mocked by the world at a cost of eighty millions [of British pounds]."[3]

The Zionists had been waging a war of terror against the British in Palestine for many years. They'd put bombs in markets, on trains, and in hotels. They'd killed many people—Arab, Jew, and Briton alike.

They hoped that if they continued harming and killing British people in occupied Palestine, the general public in Britain—the families, friends, and fellow citizens of the victims—would get so sick of the tragedies that they'd force the British government to withdraw, leaving Palestine wide open for anyone who could grab land by force. Then the Zionists would only have to fight an open war with whoever (Palestinian or Arab) was left, and take whatever they could.

The bombing of the Jerusalem Officers' Club was only one of many attacks that happened that day: there were, in fact, 16 major terror operations that Saturday.[4] The British authorities, as well as the British public, were shocked, angered, and dismayed by the ferocity and coordination of the attacks. One British newspaper ran a headline in response to the attacks: "Govern or Get Out." If occupied Palestine was going to cause such trouble for the nation of England, then many British citizens didn't want their country to be involved in occupied Palestine anymore.

The British military commander in charge of keeping the peace in occupied Palestine reacted quickly. England had learned through past encounters with terrorism that a fast response to terror activity is a fairly reliable method for catching terrorists. The very next day, at 8:00 a.m., martial law was declared. *Martial law* means that the military takes over control of running the country; the civilian government is set aside and the armed forces are put in charge of everything.

There was no mail service; no motor vehicles were permitted on the roads except those on military business; telephone service was limited; banks needed special permission to operate; the courts were taken over by the military; and all police duties were given to the armed forces.[5] In each of the two largest cities, Tel Aviv and Jerusalem, 10,000 troops were deployed to secure the area and search for terrorists. These deployments were called Operation Elephant and Operation Hippo.

Elephant and Hippo were complete failures; instead of stopping more terrorist attacks, catching terrorists, and giving civilians (in both Palestine and England) some reassurance that the terrorists would be beaten, the operations actually *increased* the terrorism problem.

The Irgun and other terrorist groups now had more targets to attack with more soldiers on the streets. A day after martial law was declared, the Irgun made three attacks, wounding nine people. The terrorists continued, often hitting targets inside the "security zones" just to prove that terror can strike anywhere, and making the authorities look foolish and powerless.

Far worse was that the Zionists made the British overreact. According to at least one source, British troops shot and killed a four-year-old girl during the first few hours after the military took over government functions.[6] Of the Zionist prisoners taken during the Elephant and Hippo operations, two killed themselves in prison,

⚕ TERROR IN OCCUPIED PALESTINE

The fight for Israeli independence was a violent, bloody struggle. Here is a cursory list of proto-Zionist terrorist attacks, which eventually resulted in an Israeli victory, and England ceding a Jewish homeland.

1931–37. The Irgun makes a series of about 60 disconnected attacks against Arab targets, many of them civilian. These include the murders of workers at a banana plantation; bombs that kill people in cafes, markets, post offices, bus/train stations, and sunbathers at a beach. Over 250 Arab civilians, and many British military and police personnel, are killed in these attacks.

November 1944. Two members of Lehi, a small Zionist terror outfit, assassinate British politician and statesman Lord Moyne, while he is in Cairo. The two are captured, put on public trial, and executed.

1945–46. The Palmach, an elite Zionist insurgency unit, carries out a host of attacks on British targets. These targets include bridges, communications and transportation centers, as well as police stations.

July 1946. The Irgun detonate a bomb inside the King David Hotel in Jerusalem, killing 91 people, most of them civilians.

1947. The Stern Gang (Lehi) uses a letter-bomb campaign to attack and harass British politicians. The group finances itself with criminal activity, and attacks British rail, petroleum, and other infrastructure targets.

May 1947. A team of Irgun paramilitary forces attacks the British prison in Acre in order to free other Irgun members.

February–March 1948. The train that ran from Cairo to Haifa was mined twice, in subsequent months. The first attack kills 28 British soldiers; the second kills 40 civilians.

and several others were able to smuggle out statements that accused their British jailers of torture and inhumane treatment. All of these things, when added to the limited government and civilian services (phones, mail, etc.), upset the rest of the general population, both in Palestine and back in England.

April 1948. Participants belonging to the Zionist Irgun and Lehi groups massacre more than 100 Arab civilians at Deir Yassin, including elderly persons, women, and children.

September 1948. Lehi operatives assassinate the United Nations mediator for peace assigned to occupied Palestine while he is in Jerusalem. Although some of those involved in the plot are captured soon thereafter, they are all later released.

Bullet-riddled cacti are seen in the village of Deir Yassin where more than 100 Palestinian Arabs, predominantly women, children, and the elderly, were massacred by Irgun-Stern raiders in April 1948. *AP*

In just 16 days, martial law ended. The British military had failed in both their objectives: to end terror and to win political victories with the Zionist populace. Some 78 suspected terrorists were captured, but about four terror attacks per *day* were committed during the operations.

Eventually, the following year, the British would leave, and the Zionists would create the country of Israel, where occupied Palestine was once located.

LESSONS LEARNED

The Irgun's goals were very similar to those of the IRB: they both wanted to create their own country (and, coincidentally, they both wanted to kick out the British). Where the IRB wanted to raise support among the citizens of Britain and Ireland, however, the Irgun wanted, instead, to disgust and shame the citizens of Britain. The Irgun created a pattern of terrorist tactics that would be followed by many other terrorist groups in the future, including some who would later operate inside the very territory that the Jews had liberated from the British: Israel.

Government

- Using overwhelming force is not always a good method for taking control of even small areas, like cities. Putting soldiers on the street to try to make things safe can provide terrorists with more targets they can shoot at, blow up, or otherwise attack.
- The counterterror fight has little to do with winning gun battles or capturing prisoners; the real fight is political. The government can win every engagement where bloodshed occurs, and still lose the war. In the end, the side that can claim victory and convince the citizens to support them will have won, regardless of who was victorious in battle.

Terrorists

- If terrorists can persuade government forces to overreact, either by angering them or committing small attacks, then the terrorists can make huge political gains with very little risk and expense. Every time a government counterterror troop shoots an innocent person, or blows up the wrong building, or in some way harms a peaceful citizen, many, many more citizens will become sympathetic to the terrorists.

■ Whenever the government makes a definite claim, such as stating, "this area is safe," terrorists can achieve major political victories by proving the government wrong. Attacking an area that the government is supposed to be protecting is a sure way of making the government look stupid and useless, and persuading the citizens of both countries (the government's homeland and the terrorists' homeland) that the terrorists are smarter, tougher, and better than the government.

■ A series of small, coordinated attacks over a short time span can be just as, if not more, effective than a single massive battle. If planned properly, the small attacks can be much safer for the terrorists, too.

■ Using a variety of regular civilians to take part in the war only on a part-time basis is incredibly effective. Almost 15 years prior to the British experience in occupied Palestine, Chinese dictator Mao Zedong had used similar tactics in his infamous "Mobile War" strategy. Mao described the ability of the terrorist to hide among the population, just like a "fish" hiding in the "sea of the people." This makes it much more difficult for government forces to find, capture, and prosecute terrorists. It also reduces the expense of maintaining a full-time fighting force, as the part timers can support themselves with their normal jobs and in their own homes.

COUNTERTERROR TACTICS

The Zionist terrorists became a model to future terrorists worldwide. They also gave their eventual homeland, Israel, an edge when it came time for the Israeli government to fight against terrorists.

Effective

■ Massive, overwhelming force used in dragnet operations, like roadblocks and house-to-house searches, can bring in many suspects, and result in the capture or killing of many terrorists.

However, this kind of operation is very expensive, and often angers the rest of the populace who aren't involved in the fight and want to go about their normal lives.

■ Monitoring communications networks, such as the telephone switches in occupied Palestine, can often give the government insight into future terrorist activity. This is expensive and time-consuming, though, as trained personnel have to listen to a lot of boring conversations just to find a small bit of important information. Current antiterror forces monitor many types of communications, including telephone, cell phone, and e-mail, and use computerized sorting programs to try to find discussions between terrorists.

Ineffective

■ Making boasts that are meant to reassure the civilians, either at home or in the occupied territory, is risky. Whether the claim was that an area was safe, or certain terrorists were captured permanently and would stand trial, or that the war will be over by a certain date, the British created opportunities for the terrorists. Whenever the government makes any claim, the government has a harder time backing it up than the terrorists do in knocking it down: the government has to prevent *every* attack, while the terrorists just need *one* successful operation to make the government look bad.

■ Controlling prisons in a secure, humane fashion is key. When word got out that prisoners were being tortured, people back in Great Britain were disgusted, and the Zionists were outraged. This only brought sympathy for the terrorists. Moreover, when the government promised that some prisoners would be brought to trial, and the prisoners succeeded in killing themselves with explosives *inside* the government's own prison, that made the government look foolish and incompetent.

■ The government can't act indiscriminately. Precision attacks are necessary for counterterror operations. The terrorists can blow up just about anyone and still be successful: the job of the terrorist is to create terror. The government, on the other hand, has to be careful not to harm or kill anyone besides terrorists, or the people on both sides get very angry and start to believe the terrorists.

- Using military forces to "keep the peace" is often not a good idea. The vast majority of military personnel are trained in how to kill people and destroy things; they are not trained in law enforcement or other security procedures. It is very likely that harm will come to civilians if the military is put in charge of looking after them.

Assassination:
Terrorist Tool

In 1950 the White House was being renovated. President Harry Truman was therefore staying at Blair House, the official guesthouse, right across the street.

On November 1, 1950, 25-year-old Griselio Torresola walked up Pennsylvania Avenue, just west of Blair House, and headed east toward the building. Thirty-six-year-old Oscar Collazo approached from the opposite side. As Collazo neared the front door, he drew a pistol and opened fire on a group of Secret Service agents and White House policemen guarding the entrance. The guards returned fire.

At the same time, Torresola ambushed two White House policemen on the other side of the entrance. One was in a guard shack; Torresola shot him three times. The other was on the steps to the basement entrance of the building. Torresola shot him thrice, also.

Torresola then turned to help his compatriot, and shot another guard across the street, hitting him in the knee. Meanwhile, Collazo was shot in the chest and head, and collapsed.

The man Torresola had shot in the guard booth, White House Police Private Leslie Coffelt, staggered to his feet. Leaning against a wall, he steadied himself enough to fire his gun at Torresola. The single shot hit Torresola in the skull, killing him instantly.

Collazo was arrested at the scene, and later recovered from his wounds. His wife, Rosa, was arrested in New York on suspicion of being an accomplice to the attack. Torresola was dead, and Private Leslie Coffelt died later that same day, succumbing to the wounds Torresola had inflicted.[1]

⚲ A BRIEF LIST OF TWENTIETH-CENTURY TERRORIST-RELATED ASSASSINATIONS AND ASSASSINATION ATTEMPTS

1968. Black civil rights leader Martin Luther King Jr. is shot in the throat by white supremacist James Earl Ray while King is standing on a hotel balcony in Memphis, Tennessee. King is pronounced dead an hour after the attack. Ray is arrested two months later and pleads guilty to charges connected to the attack. Ray hated the civil rights movement and hoped to delay or destroy it by killing King.

1981. President Ronald Reagan is shot by crazed gunman John Hinckley Jr., while leaving a Washington, D.C., hotel. Hinckley fires six times but does not directly hit Reagan; Reagan is struck by a bullet to the chest when the round bounces off the presidential limousine. Hinckley's bullets hit three other people. Hinckley is arrested at the scene, and nobody dies as a result of the attack. Hinckley is trying to convince people he is tough, smart, and dedicated, in the hopes that a woman will find him appealing.

1981. Egyptian president Mohammed Anwar Al Sadat is attacked by an assassination team of Islamic fundamentalists in the Egyptian army. The assassins storm out of a truck during a military review parade, attacking the presidential review stand with automatic rifles and hand grenades. Seven people are killed in the two-minute attack, including two of the assassins; the rest of the hit team are arrested at the scene. Sadat is declared dead soon after the attack. The terrorists are members of a movement that hates Sadat for making peace with the nation of Israel and hope the killing will increase hostility between the two countries.

1995. Israeli president Yitzhak Rabin is shot twice by Yigal Amir, a right-wing Israeli extremist who resented the fact that Rabin tried to make peace with the Palestinians. Rabin eventually dies as a result of the injuries.

Both Torresola and Collazo were born in Puerto Rico, and they had decided to assassinate President Truman in the hopes of raising public sympathy and attention to their native land, and so gain its independence.

Puerto Rico is a small island southeast of Cuba. It has belonged to the United States since 1898, when the Spanish-American War came to an end. Puerto Rico is not an American state, but neither is it a colony; it has a strange status, and is called a "commonwealth." Puerto Ricans are considered citizens of the United States in many ways, but they don't have all the same rights as other U.S. citizens (for instance, they can't vote to elect an American president).

This situation angers some Puerto Ricans, as it angered Collazo and Torresola. Both men were members of the Nationalist Party of Puerto Rico (NPR), a political group formed in the hopes of achieving Puerto Rico's independence from the United States. Over the years spanning the first half of the twentieth century, nationalists committed many terror attacks in Puerto Rico, including bombings, shootings, and robberies.

On October 30, 1950, several teams of fighters launched revolutionary attacks against targets in San Juan and Jayuya, Puerto Rico. The rebel groups included Torresola's brother and sister, both of whom were wounded, and a man known as Albizu Campos, a leader of the Nationalist Party, and the man who had been the mentor of both Collazo and Torresola. All three—Torresola's brother and sister, and Campos—were captured.

The uprising was a disaster. Most Americans didn't care: it was just another example of Latin American violence and hadn't changed anything politically, socially, or otherwise. Collazo and Torresola were anxious to act and desperate to do something, anything, that would draw the attention of the American public to Puerto Rico's desire for independence.

They decided to kill the American president.

Their plan was fairly straightforward: go to Washington, D.C., find the president, and shoot him.

It almost worked.

The security team guarding the president was poorly equipped, poorly trained, and wasn't completely capable of handling an assassination attempt, by terrorists or anyone else. There were nine armed men, a collection of Secret Service agents, and White House Police Force troops. Several of them were military combat veterans; they had all been trained with firearms. In addition to service revolvers, they had access to heavy weapons, such as riot guns and Thompson submachine guns.

The decisive factors seemed to be these: all the men on the security team were brave and dedicated, and Collazo's gun misfired when he first pulled the trigger.

The entire battle took approximately 39 seconds. During this time, the target, president of the United States Harry S. Truman, was in a second-floor bedroom that overlooked the front of Blair House, taking a nap. Truman, a military veteran himself, and certainly no coward, got out of bed when he heard the gunshots and went to the window.

Diagrammed view of the attempt to assassinate President Harry Truman. *Bettmann/Corbis*

He stood 31 feet away from Torresola; less than the distance between Torresola and the guard Torresola shot across the street.

The president was almost killed that day, and the reason for it was not anger, hatred, insanity, money, or any of the other reasons many important people and powerful politicians are killed. The reason was purely politics.

As Collazo would tell a Secret Service agent interviewing him in an ambulance leaving the crime scene: "I have no feeling of ill-will against the President . . . did not come down here to shoot Mr. Truman. I came here to kill the President of the United States."[2]

Collazo and Torresola believed that if they killed the president, it would demonstrate two things: first, it would show Americans that the Puerto Ricans were serious and that they wanted independence; second, it would show Puerto Ricans that the Americans could be seriously harmed, and that a revolution might bring about Puerto Rican freedom.

Instead, Torresola ended up dead, and Collazo was sentenced to death after being found guilty of his crimes; President Truman commuted the death sentence just a few weeks before it was carried out, in 1952, and Collazo spent 27 more years in prison. President Jimmy Carter pardoned him in 1979, and Collazo returned home to Puerto Rico, where he died in 1984.

LESSONS LEARNED

Assassination has been a political tool for thousands of years and is an important aspect of terrorism. The attempt on President Truman offers many insights into modern defense against assassination.

Government

- The marksmanship training provided to the president's guards (like most police marksmanship training at the time) was pitifully bad; the guards were trained to hit stationary targets while standing upright and using a one-handed firing stance. The terrorists had a much higher success rate in hitting their targets during the battle, mostly because they used a two-handed grip on their guns. Police handgun combat training would eventually change to a more realistic mode, using moving targets and involving different firing positions and a two-handed grip.

- Of all the participants in the gunfight, either guards or assassins, Torresola was the most effective in terms of taking adversaries out of the fight. There was one major reason for this: he kept shooting at his targets until they went down. He shot two men at least three times, and fired multiple times at other men. This method would become policy for antiterror troops; today's elite units are taught the "antiterrorist double-tap," a quick two-shot burst designed to instantly take out an opponent.

Terrorists

- No single person is completely safe from attack or assassination. If the attackers are determined, fairly smart, and willing to give up their own lives, anyone can be attacked and even killed. This has been proven time and again with assassination attempts of differing "success," both before and after the attempt on Truman. American Presidents Kennedy and Reagan, Egyptian president Anwar Sadat, Israeli president Yitzhak Rabin, and civil rights leaders Martin Luther King and Malcolm X were all shot by attackers even though they were protected by some of the best security personnel and plans in the world. (See Sidebar)

- Even an unsuccessful attempt on the life of a leader can accomplish small terrorist "victories." In the months after the attack on Blair House, Truman allowed for a general vote in Puerto Rico, letting the citizens of that island decide for themselves whether they wanted to be a separate nation or to remain a protectorate of the United States. He also decided not to run for another term as president, which at least one source suggests was partially out of guilt over the death of Private Coffelt.[3]

- Evidence suggests that the actions of Torresola and Collazo were not merely the decision of those two men, but that they were part of a larger conspiracy involving the Nationalist Party. Supposedly, five men were to take part in the attack that day, but only Torresola and Collazo showed up. While we can only guess what would have happened if the terrorists had used more assassins, terrorist groups from that point on had learned to expect that a certain number of the attacking force might not be in position at the proper date and time. (For instance, in the September 11, 2001, attacks on the United States, it is certain that at least one more terrorist was supposed to join the 19 who took part.)

COUNTERTERROR TACTICS

Government security forces have definitely changed methods and procedures over the past 100 years, especially in terms of individual personnel protection.

Effective

- Having dedicated, determined men guarding someone can make all the difference between stopping an attack and having it succeed. While Truman's guards may not have been properly trained or equipped, they saved the president's life.
- A "defense in depth" strategy is often the best means to counter security threats. This theory is designed around the notion of several different "rings" of defense measures, all sharing the same center, like a bullseye. The center of the bullseye is whatever is under protection (a person, valuable material or information, etc.). Each ring is not designed to stand alone, like a fortress wall, but to slow the attack enough to allow other resources to be brought to bear to counter the attack. On the day of the attack on Truman, there was a defense-in-depth plan, but it wasn't shared among the many security team members, and it wasn't tested. Today, defense-in-depth strategies are used for protecting just about everything of value, from people to buildings to computer systems.

Ineffective

- The security detail was outgunned. The terrorists used automatic 9-millimeter handguns, while the guards carried .38 Special revolvers. While neither weapon has a lot of "stopping power" (the capability to knock a person down, or incapacitate/ kill, with one shot), the terrorists' guns carried more ammunition and fired faster, and had a higher muzzle velocity (the speed

PUERTO RICAN TERRORISM

Puerto Rican nationalists have been behind many terrorist acts in the twentieth century. Various groups (often the same group using many names) took part in these attacks, including the Macheteros, the Fuerzas Armadas de Liberacion Nacional (FALN), the Boricua Popular Army, and Puerto Rican Popular Army.

March 1954. Four Puerto Rican terrorists fired pistols inside the U.S. Capitol building while Congress was in session. The terrorists stood in a visitors' balcony, directly overlooking the debating members of Congress. Five members of Congress were hit. Nobody was killed; all terrorists were captured and sentenced to death, but President Eisenhower commuted the sentences to 70 years of imprisonment.[5]

January 1975. The FALN set off a bomb in a busy restaurant during lunchtime in New York City; four civilians were killed and more than 50 were injured.[6]

January 1981. Terrorists using explosives destroyed several jet aircraft at the Muniz Air National Guard Base in San Juan, Puerto Rico.[7]

October 1983. Macheteros terrorists fired a Light Antitank Weapon (LAW) rocket into the federal building in Hato Rey, Puerto Rico, striking offices belonging to the United States Department of Agriculture and the FBI.[8]

January 1985. Macheteros terrorists fired another LAW rocket into a building containing offices for several federal agencies.

September 2005. Filiberto Alberto Rios, one of the founders and leaders of the Boricua Popular Army, was shot and killed by FBI agents while resisting arrest. Rios had been wanted for charges involving a bank robbery in West Hartford, Connecticut, from which he had acquired money to pay for more terror attacks. According to government sources, Rios fired 19 bullets, hitting federal agents eight times, before he was killed.[9]

at which the bullet comes out of the gun). The Secret Service (like most federal and other law enforcement organizations) would eventually shift to high-caliber automatic pistols.

■ Access to bigger and better firearms was too slow. Truman's guard detail had a locked cabinet containing riot guns and a sub-machine gun; unfortunately, during the attack, it took too long for a single Secret Service agent to get to the locker, unlock it, grab a gun, and return to the fight. Since the battle was over in less than 40 seconds, the time to acquire suitable firearms was far too great. Since then, the Secret Service and other agencies tasked with protecting people have implemented various technologies and tactics to decrease the time it takes to get heavier firepower to the fight. When President Reagan was shot in 1981, Secret Service agents almost instantly deployed Uzi submachine guns, which had been hidden inside special briefcases.

■ President Truman was only 31 feet away from the assassins. Most of the day, he was literally a stone's throw away from the public; anyone could walk by Blair House on Pennsylvania Avenue. If the terrorists had used a grenade instead of guns, they could have certainly killed the president. Almost instantly after the attack, the Secret Service changed the entire way presidential security was implemented. Armor was added to the president's limousine, along with running boards to carry Secret Service agents, and the public was kept from direct contact with the president, at least until after clearing a rigid screening process.[4]

State-On-State Terrorism

On January 23, 1968, the United States Ship *Pueblo* was floating in freezing waters about 15 miles off the coast of Wonsan, North Korea. There were a few scattered clouds in the sky, but the sun was out, making even the bitterly cold day seem pleasant.

Around noon, Quartermaster Charles Law, from his position on the flying bridge of the *Pueblo*, noticed a vessel approaching. He called for the skipper, Commander Lloyd Bucher, who was having lunch. The ship's captain soon arrived to assess the situation.

The U.S. Navy deemed the *Pueblo* a scientific craft, with a mission to collect oceanographic information. And, indeed, the *Pueblo* was equipped with some gear to gather data about the world's oceans, and two scientists to operate it. But what the *Pueblo* was really designed for was to collect intelligence information: it was a spy ship. The purpose of the *Pueblo* was to use electronic, radar, and communications snooping devices to monitor the activities and positions of North Korean and Union of Soviet Socialist Republics (U.S.S.R.) military forces, and whatever other information was available. The *Pueblo's* state-of-the-art spy technology cost $2 million in 1968, which is the equivalent of about $11 million in 2005.

Bucher and Law, therefore, had good reason to be cautious. The *Pueblo*, while technically a navy warship, had only very light armament, which wouldn't be much use in a fight. Plus, as a spy ship, the *Pueblo* wasn't exactly welcome around any hostile lands, and North Korea was definitely not a friendly country, even though the Korean War had ended in 1953.

As Bucher and Law, along with many other members of the crew, watched, the North Korean craft came closer. They could soon see that it was a military vessel — an antisubmarine boat, with four deck guns and other offensive hardware. All the deck guns were pointed at the *Pueblo*, and the Korean sailors were wearing flak jackets and helmets.

The North Korean craft closed to about 60 yards, and then started to circle the *Pueblo*. Sailors on the *Pueblo* could see four more Korean vessels headed their way, from the direction of Wonsan. Fifteen minutes later, the antisub boat signaled the *Pueblo*, demanding to know the *Pueblo's* country of origin. The *Pueblo* hoisted an American flag. The Korean boat signaled for the *Pueblo* to halt or the Koreans would open fire. The American vessel, which was already stopped in the water, signaled that it was on hydrographic duties.

The North Korean boat signaled that the *Pueblo* should follow it. The *Pueblo* signaled back that its intentions were to remain in the area, then leave on the following day. A smaller Korean patrol boat pulled up alongside the antisub craft, and armed soldiers leaped from the latter to the former. Two Soviet-made MiG jets flew over the *Pueblo* and began to circle the American boat.

The patrol boat, with its load of soldiers, approached the *Pueblo*. Sailors on the deck of the patrol craft readied ropes, which they obviously intended to throw onto the *Pueblo*, so as to tie up to the American ship. The patrol boat got within 20 yards when Bucher gave the order to engage the *Pueblo's* engines to one-third of full speed, straight ahead. The *Pueblo* signaled, "Thank you for your consideration. I am departing the area."

As the *Pueblo* moved away, the Korean boats followed from a distance. The Korean antisub boat continued to signal the *Pueblo*, ordering it to follow. The *Pueblo* ignored the orders.

The Korean craft opened fire with a 57-millimeter cannon, blasting the bridge and stack of the *Pueblo*. Bucher ordered the *Pueblo* to turn around and head in the direction the Koreans ordered, at one-third speed.

On the way, Bucher tried to stall, to give the crew of the *Pueblo* time to destroy sensitive information and equipment, so that it wouldn't fall into enemy hands. The crew were throwing stuff overboard and setting fires to burn whatever they could. The captain considered scuttling the ship—purposefully sinking it, sending it to the bottom of the ocean—but decided the procedure would take too long, the water wasn't deep enough to stop the Koreans from recovering equipment by using divers, and many of his crew would die if exposed to the freezing water.

At one point, Bucher ordered the *Pueblo* to halt, and intended to claim that the ship was crippled and could not move. The Koreans opened fire again, raking the craft with cannon and machine-gun fire. A shell passing through the middle of the boat exploded in one of the cabins, blowing the leg off one of the crew members, who would die before the ship reached land, and injuring several other crew members.

The captain gave in and ordered the vessel to follow the Koreans into the harbor. The *Pueblo* was boarded, the crew was taken

This June 2006 photo shows North Korean soldiers watching the USS *Pueblo*, which was seized by the North Korean navy off the Korean coast in January 1968. *Korea News Service/AP*

captive, and the ship impounded. The *Pueblo* had surrendered without ever firing a shot.

The Korean peninsula is a small hunk of land jutting out of the Asian landmass on the northeast tip of China and the southeast tip of Russia. It borders both those countries. During World War II, the Japanese invaded Korea and brutalized the Korean people. After the war, Korea was divided into two different nations, North Korea and South Korea, with the Soviet Union running the northern part and the United States handling things in the south.

Then, in 1950, North Korea invaded South Korea. The United Nations, led by the United States, sent in forces to repel the attackers and recapture lost ground. The Chinese and U.S.S.R. provided aid and support to the North Koreans. It was the first conventional military engagement of the Cold War period.

It lasted three years and was extremely deadly, especially for the Koreans on both sides. At the end of the war, the national borders and boundaries were the same as they had been at the beginning.

The crew of the *Pueblo* were taken to a prisoner of war (POW) camp in North Korea. They were beaten, tortured psychologically and physically, and were under continuous pressure from their captors. The officers were made to sign written confessions regarding the *Pueblo's* "illegal" activity and coerced into making recorded audio and video confessions. Many of the crew were made to attend two press conferences where members of the news media observed the crew members reciting answers to questions about the incident; the North Koreans had scripted both the questions and the answers.

Many of the crew suffered from injuries and malnutrition during this time. Some of them would carry the effects for the rest of their lives.

The North Koreans had probably attacked and captured the *Pueblo* for a number of reasons—first, because the North Koreans didn't like the United States and wanted to make America look bad. The United States is a loyal ally of South Korea and continues to station military forces in that country, protecting South Korea from North Korean invasion. This infuriated the North Koreans, who viewed America's presence as meddling in local affairs. By humiliating the United States, one of two world superpowers at the time, North Korea would be able to claim that it was one of the most powerful nations in the world.

The second likely reason the North Koreans took the *Pueblo* is because the U.S.S.R. might have asked them to. Recent evidence[1] suggests that the Soviets wanted a particular piece of code equipment from a U.S. Navy warship. They had a spy in the U.S. Navy, John Walker, who had provided them with a key for American codes. In order to make long-term code breaking even more effective, a coding machine named the KW-7 was necessary. The Soviets knew that every U.S. Navy ship had a KW-7, so they might have asked the Koreans to grab an American vessel whenever they could. The *Pueblo* happened to be in the wrong place at the wrong time. (Conversely, a less-accepted theory is that the United States government purposefully let the *Pueblo* be captured, in order to give the Koreans a coding device that the Americans could decipher.[2] This is far less likely to be true.)

Finally, it is possible that the Koreans attacked the *Pueblo* because they didn't like anyone spying on them. Most nations resent intrusive intelligence-collection, and many have taken actions to defeat spy vehicles. The U.S.S.R. shot down an American U-2 spy plane in 1960, taking the pilot prisoner. In 1962, Cuba shot down another U-2, killing the pilot. In 1967, Israeli aircraft and missile boats fired on the USS *Liberty*, a spy ship very similar to the *Pueblo*, killing 34 personnel and wounding 173 others. A Chinese Air Force fighter plane accidentally collided with an American EP-3E aircraft in 2001, forcing the Americans to land on Hainan Island. The Chinese kept the crew for 10 days, and the plane for several months.

Of course, the most probable explanation is that the Koreans attacked and captured the *Pueblo* for a combination of all these reasons.

If the cause of the *Pueblo* incident was primarily a means for the Soviets to grab a KW-7 coding unit, then it was not a terrorist act; it was an act of robbery. But the other reasons suggest an example of state-on-state terrorism, or one nation committing a terrorist act against another in order to achieve political goals.

In terms of our definition of terrorism, the *Pueblo* incident was an illegal act (seizing the ship of another nation in international waters), using force (guns and cannon were employed), against a small number of people (the crew of the *Pueblo*), in order to accomplish political goals (either halting spying or raising public opinion of North Korea's power), by persuading a large number of people (either the governments of the world or the American people), to change political policies or ideas (getting America to recognize North Korea's power, or at least to stop spy missions near North Korea).

The North Koreans refuted that the act was in any way illegal: they claimed that the *Pueblo* had violated North Korean territory by sailing too close to the coast. Different sources mention that North Korea had notions about what "international waters" meant that conflicted with those of most other nations. To most countries, the ocean 12 or more miles from the coast of a country is considered "international waters" and belongs to no single nation. Under the Law of the Sea (a set of treaties between most of the world's nations governing how ships and shipping are to be treated legally), all maritime craft are allowed to operate in international waters without fear of harassment or harm. Even those ships that do break the 12-mile limit are not to be attacked instantly, but, instead, are to be warned and escorted back out to sea. In 1968 North Korea had not signed the Law of the Sea treaty, and may have claimed a 50-mile territorial limit for itself.

In any event, firing on the naval craft of another nation without provocation is certainly an act of war and is illegal during peacetime.

The North Koreans tried for many months to make political use of the *Pueblo* and its crew. North Korea gained quite a bit of publicity and notoriety worldwide. Americans were scared and angered by the surprise attack. What North Korea seemed to crave the most, more than any other item during negotiations for the release of the ship and crew, was a formal apology from the United States government and a promise never to send spy ships near North Korea again.

In December of 1968, 11 months after the *Pueblo* had been taken, North Korea got what it had demanded. Representatives of the United States signed a document admitting that the *Pueblo* was a spy ship, that it had violated the territory of North Korea, and that America would never do such a thing again. The surviving crew of the *Pueblo* were released to South Korea and returned home soon thereafter.

Immediately upon return of the crew, the United States made an announcement that the apology was worthless and that America would continue any naval operations the American government deemed necessary.

All members of the *Pueblo's* crew were debriefed at great length by American investigators in order to determine the cause and blame for the incident. The findings of a U.S. Navy court of inquiry included a recommendation to court martial Bucher and at least one other officer. The Secretary of the Navy declined that suggestion and absolved Bucher of ultimate blame. Bucher finished out his military career.

LESSONS LEARNED

Nations have long conducted acts of terrorism against each other. The *Pueblo* incident gives countries an excellent example of state-on-state terrorism from which to learn how to deal with similar future situations.

♀ THE *MAYAGUEZ* INCIDENT

In 1975 Cambodian naval forces attacked and captured the SS *Mayaguez*, an American cargo ship operating in international sea lanes. Supposedly, the Cambodians believed the ship was transporting equipment that might be used to attack Asian countries and wanted to send a message to America that it should cease meddling in the region. The *Mayaguez* was taken to a Cambodian port and the 39 members of the crew were removed from the boat.

Three days later, President Gerald Ford ordered the military to stage a rescue mission. Over a dozen aircraft, including rescue helicopters, fighter planes, and a gunship, took part in the operation, as did a navy frigate and destroyer, and hundreds of marines. The *Mayaguez* was retaken, but the crew had been moved to another Cambodian port.

During the rescue attack, the *Mayaguez* crew were released by the Cambodians and sent away on a Thai fishing boat, to be taken to a U.S. Navy ship nearby.

Eighteen American military service members were killed in the rescue operation, and 23 died during earlier missions in support of the rescue.

Government (victim of terrorist attack)

- Planning and practicing the destruction of sensitive material before an attack takes place is critical. During the *Pueblo* incident, the crew was hampered in their destructive activities by lack of time, poor destruction equipment, and the realities of the situation which hadn't been considered when making the destruction plan. For example, the room that required the most destruction wasn't large enough for the sailors to effectively swing the big sledgehammers, which were their main destruction tools.

- The enemy nation, in making a terrorist attack, may be acting in an irrational manner, and have a very different view of the situation before, during, and after the event. The North Koreans were very concerned about certain elements of the negotiation to release the *Pueblo* crew, such as the size and shape of the negotiation table, and the wording of the "apology," while the American negotiators didn't care at all about North Korea's concerns, which they considered trivial, and only wanted the crew back. Also, the North Koreans never admitted wrongdoing and forced the Americans to accept blame for the event.

Terrorists (government making the attack)

- Surprise and overwhelming force are extremely effective weapons. Even though both the USS *Liberty* and the USS *Banner*, ships with roles very similar roles to the *Pueblo*, had been harassed, threatened, or attacked by Chinese, Israeli, and Soviet forces, repectively, the *Pueblo's* crew and captain never considered that the ship would actually be attacked until the attack was already happening. By that point, the *Pueblo* was ready to surrender, as resistance would have been useless.

- Knowledge of the culture you are attacking is important. Even while the crew of the *Pueblo* were being forced to participate in propaganda favorable to the Koreans, the American prisoners still fought back in quiet, subtle ways. For instance, the sailors raised their middle fingers in every photograph the North Koreans took, explaining to their captors that it was a Hawaiian good luck sign. Eventually, the North Koreans figured out what "flipping the bird" meant, and punished the crew for it.[3]

COUNTERTERROR TACTICS

Even when faced with the potential and possibility for state-on-state terror activity, a government can protect itself and even preempt that kind of attack.

Effective

- The American public (one of the main targets of the North Korean terrorist effort), by and large, did not side with or feel sympathy for the Koreans. Korean efforts to continually portray the American Navy and government as the aggressors in the *Pueblo* incident mostly fell flat. Korean propaganda largely missed the mark in terms of convincing the American people that the American military was violating international law or custom. This was mostly because the crew of the *Pueblo* were effective at communicating to the outside world how they were being treated.

Ineffective

- Training your personnel to resist interrogation, propaganda efforts, and the drudgery and boredom of captivity is important. Morale can be a decisive factor in not only maintaining a sense of loyalty and commitment, but even survival. Only two members of *Pueblo*'s crew had completed the military's Survival, Evasion, Resistance, and Escape (SERE) training, and even they felt that the training had been somewhat inadequate. After the *Pueblo* incident, the U.S. military enhanced the training course with lessons learned from the survivors and a better idea of what to expect in future, similar situations.

Non-State Actors Terrorizing Civilians

The ship was almost empty. The cruise began with almost 700 passengers, but on October 7, 1985, most of them had gotten out at Alexandria and would tour a small part of Egypt, rejoining the boat at Port Said. Less than 100 passengers had chosen to remain on board.

There were four men on board who weren't passengers or crew members. These men were members of a group called the Palestine Liberation Front (PLF). They were heavily armed and had been trained in paramilitary operations.

The men were waiting for the ship to leave Egyptian waters; they wanted to sneak into Israel, the ship's ultimate destination. But they were surprised when the ship's crew discovered their weapons, and the terrorists were forced to act ahead of schedule. They stormed the engine room and the bridge of the ship, firing their weapons into the bulkheads in order to shock and frighten the crew into submission.

The next day, having secured control of the craft, the terrorists radioed to authorities on the shore. The terrorists wanted Israel to release 50 Palestinian militants being held in Israeli prisons. Then the boat disappeared. By pushing out into the open waters of the Mediterranean Sea, where a lot of international shipping takes place, the terrorists were able to make the *Achille Lauro* blend in and hide from the detection of governments who might attack and punish the terrorists.

And there were plenty of governments who wanted to act, too. The cruise ship belonged to an Italian company, so Italy had a claim on the fate of the vessel. England and the United States had citizens on board as passengers, so those countries had valid claims on whatever action might be performed. The boat was captured in Egyptian waters, so Egypt conceivably had a stake in the outcome as well.

Each nation's security, military, intelligence, and command teams were meeting to discuss possible courses of action, but most of those nations weren't talking to each other. There were various political reasons why the different nations wouldn't communicate

Released hostages of the *Achille Louro* liner hijacking being taken ashore after the four Palestinian hijackers surrendered. *Bernard Bisson/Sygma/Corbis*

and cooperate, and this situation became more complicated as the hijacking continued and even more countries became involved.

The following day, the ship showed up at the Syrian port of Tartus, where the terrorists requested docking services. The Italian and American governments put pressure on the Syrian government, asking that the ship not be allowed to land. The Syrians agreed with the Italians and Americans, and the ship left Syrian waters that night.

On the third day of the event, the ship was back in Egyptian waters; the Americans asked the Egyptians not to let the boat into Egyptian territory, but the Italians, at this point, didn't object. The Egyptians let the *Achille Lauro* anchor off the coast, near Port Said.

A delegation of Egyptian and Palestinian negotiators went out to the ship on a small boat. By that afternoon they reached a settlement: the terrorists would surrender the ship and all the people aboard; in return, the terrorists would be turned over to the custody of the Palestinian Liberation Organization (PLO). The terrorists rode an Egyptian Navy boat back into Port Said and were taken into custody by the Egyptians.

At this point the American government learned that the night before, while the *Achille Lauro* was in Syrian waters, and refused entry into a Syrian port, the terrorists had murdered a crippled American citizen, and thrown his body and wheelchair overboard.

Terrorists take civilians hostage for several reasons. It makes the terrorists seem more frightening, more deadly, because if it appears that they're willing to attack unarmed, untrained civilians, then they are willing to attack anyone. Also, civilians are usually easier to take and keep captive; they don't typically fight back or try to escape or struggle with their captors. Finally, governments are often less inclined to attempt armed rescue missions when civilian hostages are present because of the danger that the hostages might be killed in the crossfire. Indeed, there are very few hostage-rescue operations involving civilians that don't result in the loss of innocent victims (see Sidebar).

But once the decision-makers in the United States government learned that the PLF terrorists who had taken the *Achille Lauro* had murdered an American citizen, they were forced to act. Only a few months prior, a commercial aircraft had been hijacked, and an

American citizen (a U.S. Navy service member) was tortured and murdered. The United States government wanted to send a message: American citizens could not be murdered with impunity.

According to many reports, the American government asked the Egyptian government for assistance in apprehending the terrorists. The Egyptian government declined, claiming that the terrorists

Youssef Magied al-Molqi, the Palestinian terrorist convicted of killing American citizen Leon Klinghoffer during the hijacking of the *Achille Lauro* cruise liner, is shown behind bars at the time of his trial in Genoa in May 1986. *AP*

had already fled the country. Through various intelligence-gathering methods (purportedly including electronic surveillance of the Egyptian president's office), the American government was able to determine that the Egyptians were lying. The terrorists were still in Egypt and would be flown to Tunisia later that night. Intelligence even revealed the type of aircraft, the tail number, and the airfield the terrorists would be leaving from. The Boeing 737 in which the terrorists were scheduled to ride would also carry Egyptian military personnel and some of the Palestinian negotiators who had taken part in the discussion to get the *Achille Lauro* released.

The Americans scrambled two F-14 long-range fighter jets and an E-2C Hawkeye command-and-control aircraft.[1] The three planes conducted some extremely dangerous operations: nighttime intercepts of large aircraft, without knowing the target's exact takeoff time, course, heading, and altitude. The F-14s intercepted three incorrect targets before they found the 737 they were looking for.

The navy pilots were able to convince the 737 to divert and land in Sigonella, Sicily (part of Italy), at a base used by the North Atlantic Treaty Organization (NATO), of which both the United States and Italy are members. On the ground, American special operations forces and Italian military and police troops surrounded the plane.

Eventually, the Italian commander of Sigonella and an Egyptian diplomat were able to gain access to the 737 and convince the Egyptian military personnel to release the terrorists into Italian custody.[2]

LESSONS LEARNED

Hijacking was nothing new when the capture of the *Achille Lauro* took place; terrorists attacking and killing civilians wasn't a new idea, either. In this particular case, however, many governments were able to act together to resolve the situation using many methods, including military intervention, which makes the *Achille Lauro* situation exceptional.

Government

- Many governments walk a fine line between wanting to appear tough, so that potential terrorists won't attack, and wanting to

appear fair, so that terrorists won't be given an additional justifi-
cation to attack. The United States encountered problems associated with this balance during the *Achille Lauro* event: many
of the nations involved, such as Egypt and Italy, did not want to
appear either weak or unfair. These governments did not grant

⚲ RESCUE MISSIONS

Because of cases like the *Achille Lauro*, governments often choose
to attack terrorists, even if they are holding hostages. Here is
a partial list of some terrorist acts that ended with military
intervention.

July 3, 1976. Israeli commandos attack Entebbe Airport in
Uganda. Terrorists sympathetic to the Palestinian independence movement had hijacked a French airliner a week
prior and forced it to land at Entebbe. The terrorists, with
the cooperation of the Ugandan government, released
all passengers who were not Jews or Israelis, and then
demanded the release of their compatriots, imprisoned
Palestinian terrorists held by several different countries.
The Israeli commandos strike in a fast, methodical, and
secretive manner, which becomes the template for all
future military counterterror intervention activities. One
hostage is killed in the raid, one hostage who had been
taken to another site is killed in reprisal, one Israeli soldier
is killed, six hijackers are killed, and about 45 Ugandan
soldiers, who tried to stop the Israelis' escape are killed.

April 24, 1980. Eight American military service members die
during an aborted rescue attempt in Iran. Iranian extremists, while protesting American involvement in Iran's
politics, had taken over the United States embassy in
Tehran, Iran's capital, in November 1979, capturing some
53 Americans and holding them hostage. President Jimmy
Carter authorized Operation Eagle Claw, sending U.S. military forces into Iran to free the hostages. After a series of
mistakes and unlucky circumstances, two helicopters and
a transport plane collide and explode, killing eight aircrew
members. The kidnappers eventually free the hostages in
January 1981.

every American request or demand, in order to appear strong and fair. This can make American responses to terrorist activity much more difficult.

■ Questions of law and legality become very important when the borders and property and citizens of different countries are

May 5, 1980. Members of the British Special Air Service (SAS) Counterrevolutionary Warfare (CRW) unit storm the Iranian embassy in London, which is held by a group of Iraq-trained terrorists. The terrorists demand independence for a small region of Iran, but it later turns out that the gunmen mainly intended to embarrass and humiliate the Iranian government (Iraq and Iran were at war at the time). One hostage is killed in the attack and five of the six terrorists are killed. The remaining terrorist is captured and imprisoned; he was sentenced to life in prison.

November 25, 1985. EgyptAir Flight 648 is hijacked by three Palestinian terrorists and forced to land in Malta, an island in the Mediterranean Sea. One terrorist is killed on board by an EgyptAir security officer, who is himself subsequently killed. After the terrorists shoot and kill a number of passengers, Egyptian special forces rush the aircraft. In the battle, 56 hostages and one terrorist are killed. The remaining terrorist is captured and sentenced to 25 years in a Maltese prison. He is released after eight years, but recaptured and brought to the United States, where is he sentenced to life imprisonment in 1996 for killing Americans during the hijacking.[3]

September 1, 2004. Some 30 Chechen terrorists take over a Russian school in Beslan, holding about 1,200 people hostage, most of them children. The terrorists demand independence for Chechnya, a Russian province. After three days, Russian security forces exchange gunfire with the terrorists, and chaos ensues. More than 300 civilians are killed, more than half of them children.

involved. In the *Achille Lauro* case, the event included an Italian ship with American passengers in Egyptian and Syrian waters, an Egyptian airliner, and an international air base on Italian soil. Even if there is a solution that seems to be useful (like having jet fighters force down the 737), some of the governments involved have to be careful, or risk setting "precedent." The concept of *precedent* means that because something was allowed in the past, then it might be done again. If, for instance, Italy allowed American military forces to kidnap foreigners on Italian soil once, then Italy might be expected to allow such behavior in the future. Italy, for one, was concerned with this type of question. The *Achille Lauro* event forced many governments to reconsider laws associated with trespassing, the use of military forces, and terrorism.

TERRORISTS

- While the threat of harming civilians is an extremely powerful terrorist tool, actually harming a civilian can turn public sentiment against terrorists. It can also spur antiterrorist forces (and the government decision-makers who run them) into action, where they'd otherwise be unlikely to intervene.

COUNTERTERROR TACTICS

When responding to the *Achille Lauro* incident, military forces encountered some new situations that taught them how to deal with future terrorist activities involving civilians.

Effective

- Sometimes the use of overwhelming military force can be quite effective. The United States was able to deploy and operate an aircraft carrier and many other naval craft, jet fighters, and ground personnel in a very rapid fashion. This gives decision makers a lot of options for dealing with terrorists, including the option to attack.
- Terrorists often use hostages as bargaining pieces, threatening to harm or kill them if the government does not comply with the

terrorists' demands. But because of incidents like the *Achille Lauro*, governments put serious consideration into using military force. Many figure that if hostages are going to be killed by terrorists, it is perhaps best, from a political perspective, to try to intervene, and perhaps prevent the deaths of hostages, or at least minimize any hostage casualties. There are conflicting opinions about this idea. Some experts suggest that more hostages are killed in "rescue" missions than the terrorists would kill themselves. (See Sidebar)

Ineffective

■ When conflicting jurisdictions and law enforcement entities are involved, it can sometimes be difficult to obtain "justice." Because there are so many international considerations, terrorists may be treated in a way that would otherwise be seen as inappropriate. For instance, in the *Achille Lauro* situation, the Egyptians allowed a PLF terrorist planner, Abu Abbas, access to the terrorists on board the ship, first via radio and telephone, then, eventually, in person. After the 737 was forced down in Italy, the Italians allowed Abbas to leave the country, even though he was later indicted of terrorist crimes *in absentia* (while he was not present in court). The other terrorists were treated in what might be considered strange ways, also: two were paroled a little over five years after the event, and another was released after serving only 10 years of a 30-year sentence.

State-Sponsored Terrorism

On December 21, 1988, Pan American World Airways Flight 103 was late departing Heathrow International Airport in London, England, but then, many flights are. It's not uncommon for an aircraft, even an America-bound 747 jumbo jet, to spend a half-hour or more on the taxiways waiting for approval to take off.

The plane quickly climbed, going all the way up to 31,000 feet in about 20 minutes. It headed northeast over Scotland on its way to New York. As it crossed into Scottish airspace, the plane became the responsibility of a Scottish air controller, Alan Topp.

Topp communicated with the plane, verifying that the 747 was doing everything that it should, and giving it directions for its flight path. Then Topp focused his attention on another aircraft in the area for a few moments.

When Topp looked back at his radar screen, the little green "+" sign that represented Pan Am 103 was still there, still doing what it was supposed to do. He watched it for a few more moments—then, it just disappeared. Instead, there were now four or five tiny green blips, all of them twinkling.

In the small town of Lockerbie, Scotland, most of the people were just settling in to spend the cold evening at home with family or friends. It's an old, quiet village, with hundreds of years of history, but fewer than 5,000 people. At just after 7:00 p.m., pieces of Pan Am 103 came raining down on Lockerbie. Eleven of the town's residents died in the blazing storm of shrapnel and the ensuing explosions and fires.

This December 1988 photo shows wrecked houses and a deep crater in the ground in the village of Lockerbie, Scotland. The damage was caused by the crash of Pan Am Flight 103 on December 21, 1988. *Martin Cleaver/AP*

A small amount of explosives, probably a pound or less, blew a hole in the left front section of the plane, almost at the bottom of the aircraft. There was a bomb in the luggage compartment, inside a suitcase, hidden inside a portable radio; it detonated, creating the hole. The hole caused the plane to rip itself to pieces, as the speed of the plane and the friction of the air worked like a shredder. This force combined with the shock waves of the explosion and tore the plane apart in seconds.

Emergency personnel and investigators were on the scene almost immediately. Because the crash involved an American plane bound for America with many American passengers, the investigators included not only British law enforcement personnel and aircraft regulators, but also American diplomats and an FBI agent stationed in England. Soon thereafter, American investigators and forensic experts based in the United States joined them.

Hundreds of searchers combed through the countryside surrounding Lockerbie. The altitude and speed of Pan Am 103 had spread wreckage and bodies over 81 miles. Every piece had to be collected and analyzed to determine what had caused the massive plane to come apart and fall. According to one person present, the search team was told to gather everything they found: "If it's not a rock, and it's not growing, pick it up and put it in a bag."[1]

Experts combed through each bit of wreckage, looking for telltale signs of equipment malfunction or an explosion. Then, even before a determination was made, each bit of wreckage was moved to a location where the fuselage of the plane would be reassembled to get a better idea of what had happened. For the size of the job, the results came pretty quickly. Just five days after Pan Am 103 was blown out of the sky, investigators had positive proof that a bomb was involved.

Two particular aspects gave them certainty. The first was the condition of certain pieces of wreckage that had been shattered and fragmented, as only occurs with an explosion. The second took a bit more science and time. British forensic experts checked the pieces of metal that had been closest to the explosion and found traces of Semtex, an explosive.

With confirmation that the plane and passengers had fallen victim to a terrorist attack, most of the world's law enforcement and intelligence agencies kicked into full gear. The British, American, and German services had started investigating when the news of the loss of Pan Am 103 first broke. They were already doing background work to see if they could figure out what group or individual would have the motive or opportunity to destroy an American aircraft. (Pan Am 103 had begun its final trip in West Germany.)

A forensics explosives laboratory photograph shows recovered fragments of a suitcase that contained a bomb that exploded aboard the Pan Am airliner above Lockerbie, Scotland, in December 1988. Reuters/Corbis

The counterterror and counterintelligence branches of most of the world's governments started sifting through the mountains of information they'd gathered over the years. As more evidence was collected and more information came in, the agencies conferred with each other, trading leads and offering suggestions.

The first real lead (after investigators followed many false ones) came from Germany. A suspected terrorist bomb maker had been picked up, along with many other suspected terrorists and conspirators, in a massive, nationwide sweep only two months before Pan Am 103's fall. The bomb maker not only had possession of Semtex, the same type of explosive used in the bombing, but also had a bomb disguised as the same kind of radio that had blown up Pan Am 103.

It appeared the man in question and some of his cohorts were members of a Palestinian terrorist organization, possibly Hezbollah. The investigators dug further, while wreckage was still being pulled out of the land surrounding Lockerbie.

The more debris that was picked up from the remains of Pan Am 103, the more leads the investigators got. The next new piece of evidence was a piece of clothing.

Explosions are strange; blast forces can be quirky and very unpredictable. The decisive piece of clothing found near Lockerbie demonstrates that. It was a baby's jumpsuit, almost totally intact, with the manufacturer's tag still attached. Chemical residues proved that it had to be contained in the same piece of luggage that the bomb was in when it went off. That it survived intact is an example of how bizarre blast dynamics can be.

The clothing tag led investigators to a small clothing company in Malta where the jumpsuit was made and sold. A company representative there not only remembered the batch of jumpsuits the Pan Am 103 evidence came from, but he remembered the man who probably bought that particular one. The customer had purchased a variety of strange clothing, including children's clothes, none of which were the same size, which made the salesman suspicious. The customer had also purchased an umbrella and a certain type of coat, the salesman remembered.

Back in England, the search and collection team had been cataloging the thousands of pieces of debris that were the remains of Pan Am 103. All the data was put into a computer, where it could be cross-referenced and checked. When investigators queried the database for any pieces of umbrella or that kind of coat, they found the

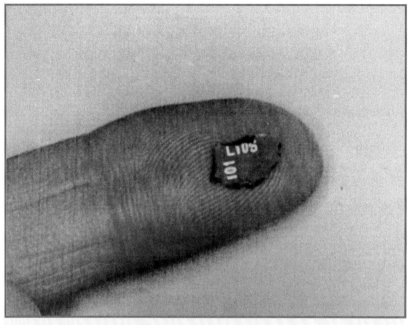

This fragment of the bomb timer, smaller than a fingernail, proved to be crucial in tracking down the people responsible for the Pan Am 103 bombing. *Justice Department/AP*

pieces in the inventory. Then those pieces were sent to the forensic lab for further analysis.

All the pieces had traces of Semtex and other chemical indications. They had been in the terrorist's suitcase, along with the baby's jumper and the bomb.

The Maltese salesman provided investigators with a description of the customer and also stated that the man in question had a Libyan accent. The Libyan connection was particularly fascinating because of another piece of evidence found at the crash scene.

Searchers had found a one-half inch piece of circuit board wedged into a piece of clothing. They couldn't identify it immediately, so they had it inspected by British and American explosives specialists. It turned out to be a piece of a timer used in delayed bombs.

This particular timer was similar to one found in the possession of a Libyan intelligence operative who had been arrested in Senegal almost a year before Pan Am 103 was struck. The Libyan agent had been carrying Semtex, TNT, and the telltale timer.

Investigators then directed questions to the timer manufacturer, located in Switzerland. Could the timer vendor possibly identify the person or entity that purchased the very timer used on Pan Am 103 using just the tiny fragment found among the debris of the plane?

The Swiss company that made the timers was incredibly helpful. With only the piece supplied by investigators, company representatives were able to identify one of the purchasers, a man named Megrahi, who worked for the Libyan government. This seemed to be the climax of the investigation: Megrahi matched the description of the customer who had purchased the baby clothes in the Malta shop.

Two Libyan men, Megrahi and his supposed accomplice, were indicted by courts in both the United States and Great Britain in 1991. After a lot of arguing and demands, in 1999, Libya agreed to extradite the two suspects to a court in the Netherlands. In May 2000 their trial began.

In January 2001 Megrahi was found guilty of multiple counts of murder; his codefendant was acquitted and released. Megrahi lost an attempt at appeal and is currently serving a life sentence in a prison in Glasgow, Scotland.

Possibly the most fascinating aspect of this particular case was another result: the Libyan government took full blame and responsibility for the bombing of Pan Am 103 because Megrahi was a Libyan intelligence agent and he was found guilty. Libya agreed to pay around $2.7 billion in restitution to the families of the victims. In return, Libya requested that trade sanctions against Libya imposed by the United States and the United Nations be lifted.

This was a remarkable set of circumstances. A sovereign nation (Libya) contracted with non-nation-state organizations and personnel (possibly Hezbollah) to conduct a terrorist action against civilians (the crew and passengers of Pan Am 103), and then paid for the crime when it was discovered and proven. While it is very likely that other countries had used terrorists as contract killers before (and since), this case may have set the legal precedent for all cases that would follow: any nation trying to hide violent acts behind third-party terrorists would ultimately be held responsible.

⚲ A BRIEF LIST OF HIJACKINGS

When someone illegally takes control of an aircraft, it's called *hijacking*, or, sometimes, *skyjacking*. In the latter half of the twentieth century, this became a rather popular terrorist tactic, especially in the 1970s. Here is a sample of some of those incidents.

August 1969. Two Palestinian terrorists hijack TWA Flight 840 from Athens and force it to land in Damascus, Syria. Nobody is killed or injured, but the terrorists try to blow up the plane while it is on the ground. The nose of the aircraft is destroyed.

September 1970. In the span of three days, five jet airliners (leaving from Frankfurt, Zurich, Amsterdam, Tel Aviv, and Bahrain) are hijacked by members of a Palestinian terrorist group known as the PFLP (the "Popular Front for the Liberation of Palestine"). Three planes are taken to a remote Jordanian airstrip known as Dawson's Field, one is taken to Cairo, and the other lands in London when the terrorists onboard are neutralized by security forces (one is killed, the other captured). The terrorists demand that many of their imprisoned colleagues (including the terrorist captured in London) be released from countries around the world. The passengers and crew are briefly held hostage, then released a few days afterward. All four terrorist-controlled aircraft are then blown up on September 12, 1970, in front of television news cameras.

February 1974. American Samuel Byck attempts to hijack an aircraft at Baltimore-Washington International Airport in order to fly it into the White House and kill then-President Richard Nixon. Byck shoots three people and gains control of the cockpit of a DC-9 before he is shot and killed.

June 1976. Entebbe crisis (see Sidebar, Chapter 6).

September 1977. Japanese Airlines Flight 472 from Paris is hijacked by five members of the Japanese Red Army terrorist organization after a stop in Mumbai. The plane, carrying approximately 150 people, is forced to land in

Bangladesh. The terrorists demand millions of dollars in cash and the release of nine of their colleagues from Japanese prisons. Within five days, the Japanese government delivers the money and six of the prisoners; the plane is eventually taken to Algeria, where the terrorists turn the aircraft over to authorities and free the hostages.

October 1977. Lufthansa Flight 181 is hijacked by four PFLP terrorists on its way from Mallorca, working in conjunction with a German terrorist entity known as the Red Army Faction (aka, the Baader-Meinhof Gang). The terrorists demand money and the release of some Baader-Meinhof members held in a German prison. The terrorists take the plane to several different cities in different countries; sometimes they are allowed to land, sometimes not. After one particularly tense landing, the terrorists kill one of the pilots. German and British counterterror forces (German GSG9 and British SAS) storm the plane, killing three of the terrorists, capturing the other, and freeing all of the remaining hostages successfully.

December 1977. Malaysian Airlines Flight 653 is hijacked soon after takeoff from a Malaysian airport by persons and for reasons unknown, and subsequently crashes, killing all 100 people on board.

June 1985. TWA Flight 847 is hijacked en route from Athens by two Lebanese men who are later joined by a dozen more gunmen when the aircraft lands in Beirut to refuel. The hijackers demand the release of several Lebanese prisoners held by Israel, a cessation of Israeli military activity in Lebanon, and condemnation of United States involvement in the Middle East, including a car bomb allegedly set by the CIA the previous March. An American military service member on board the aircraft is beaten and killed. After two weeks and many flights between Beirut and Algiers, the hostages are released with no further casualties. Israel releases more than 700 prisoners the following month.

LESSONS LEARNED

The case of Pan Am 103 certainly changed the way the world viewed state-sponsored terrorism; in fact, it was one of the acts that gave us that term. Governments and terrorists both had to deal with the consequences of this act, also known as "The Lockerbie Bombing."

Government (victims of terrorist attack)

- Trained, experienced experts in highly specialized fields, such as blast forensics and air-disaster investigation, are invaluable when it comes to catching and prosecuting terrorist perpetrators. Knowing someone performed a terrorist act is one thing; being able to prove it in court is another.
- International cooperation is key. Countries have certain strengths to offer an investigation. For the Pan Am 103 incident, the United States provided the world's best air-mishap expert, while Great Britain lent the use of the world's finest forensic laboratory. There were situations where lack of cooperation slowed the investigation, and more than once some governments were embarrassed that they had not shared information earlier, information which may have prevented the attack (or at least helped to prevent it). Because of that embarrassment, those governments did not share information with the investigators right away, thus delaying progress of the investigation.

Terrorists (perpetrators of terrorist attack)

- Engaging in terror activities can be very expensive. The "secret" operations of Megrahi ended up costing Libya not only the amount that country paid to the victims' families, but also all the trade revenue lost during the period that international sanctions were in effect.
- Even trace amounts of evidence can lead investigators to criminals, and prosecutors to convictions. Today's technology is so amazingly exact that the smallest particles of evidence are readily identifiable and understood.

COUNTERTERROR TACTICS

Knowing how the Pan Am 103 terrorists operated, law enforcement and intelligence operatives can better secure current airline flights against bomb threats or help them capture the bombers after an attack has occurred.

Effective

- Assigning enough investigators, with a budget large enough, to track down every clue (including all the wrong ones), no matter where they might lead. Many investigators had to travel to foreign countries and spend a lot of time searching in places that turned out to be useless, but that was necessary to narrow down the clues to the ones that were real and important.

Ineffective

- Policies that aren't followed are useless. At the time of the attack on Pan Am 103 (and probably still today), the American government had a rule: no two senior intelligence officers, especially those from the same station, would travel on the same commercial airliner. This shrunk a couple of risks: first, that an accident involving that aircraft would cripple the station where those agents were assigned, and, second, that such valuable personnel would make the plane (and its passengers) a massive terrorist target. Unfortunately, several people traveling on Pan Am 103 violated that rule: the CIA's deputy station chief for Beirut and a DIA officer tasked to Beirut, plus their bodyguards. While the Libyans probably did not choose to attack Pan Am 103 because these people were on board, it was a negligent, foolish decision to have them travel together.
- Using violence to stop violent terrorist attacks seems extremely ineffective. In April 1986 the United States conducted a large-scale air raid against Libyan targets as revenge for several prior terrorist attacks thought to be sponsored by Libya. In all, five targets were hit, including the home of Libyan leader Moham-mar Khadafy. Khadafy's adopted daughter, 15-month-old Hanna, was killed, and two of Khadafy's sons were wounded. Instead of showing Khadafy that his support of worldwide terrorism would

lead to the destruction of Libya, the attack instead spurred Khadafy to *increase* his support of terror groups and activities, finally culminating in the attack on Pan Am 103. It is interesting to note that Libya eventually abandoned terrorism as a policy tool, not because of violent retaliatory attacks, but after trade sanctions and successful public prosecution of Libyan intelligence agents involved in the Pan Am 103 attack. In fact, Libya renounced the September 11, 2001, terrorist attacks on the United States and began cooperating in the global war on terror. In 2006, the American government took Libya off the list of "state sponsors of terrorism."[2]

Total War— Weapons of Mass Destruction

On the morning of March 20, 1995, five men boarded various Tokyo subway trains during rush hour, when the trains were full of commuters. Each of the men carried an umbrella and a newspaper. All of the men were scientists, doctors, or engineers. Some of the men wore surgical masks, which covered both nose and mouth, which is a fairly common practice in many parts of Asia.

All of them also carried plastic packets full of liquid sarin, a diabolical poison.

The trains were scheduled to arrive at the same place: Kasumigaseki Station, in the center of one of the city's busiest areas. Kasumigaseki is located right in the middle of many government offices and major businesses.

Each man waited until the trains were well on their way, then they dropped the newspaper they carried; folded between the sheets of the newspapers were the small plastic bags containing the sarin. Just before the train came to a halt at a station somewhere between where the men had boarded and Kasumigaseki, each man jabbed the newspaper with the end of his umbrella, puncturing the plastic bag and releasing the liquid. Then, as the train stopped, the men got off, leaving the liquid to spill across the floor of the subway car. As the men were getting into escape vehicles driven by fellow conspirators, the liquid was turning into a deadly, transparent, silent cloud: nerve gas, an insidious weapon of mass destruction.

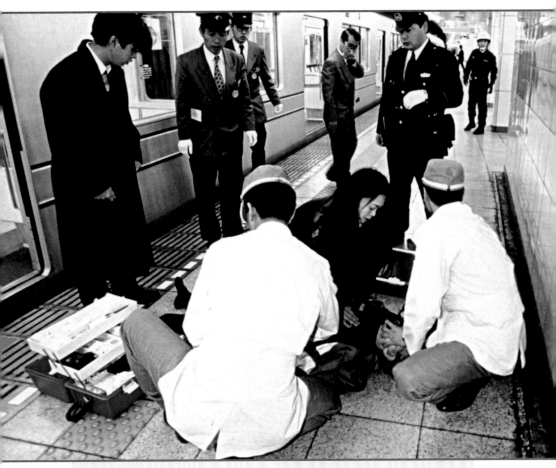

Medical personnel attend to a victim of the sarin gas attack in the Tokyo metro. *Tokyo Shimbun/Corbis Sygma*

Within minutes of each man's attack, subway riders succumbed to the invisible vapors. People were choking, coughing, and fighting the effects of nausea. Some collapsed. Hours later, 12 people were dead and thousands injured by the gas attack.

Sarin is an extremely deadly nerve agent; just milligrams can kill a person, and even a lesser dose can cause permanent brain damage, coma, and blindness.[1]

The attack on the Tokyo subway system was the work of a single group called "Aum Shinrikyo," a Japanese religion. The men involved were all trusted, highly placed members of the religion, and each was incredibly devoted to the leader, Shoko Asahara.

Asahara believed he was either a deity or the prophet of a deity, that the end of the world was coming soon, and that the United States would destroy Japan by using nerve gas. He was also the victim of glaucoma, a disease that struck him soon after he was born, leaving him blind in one eye and with only partial sight in the other.

But Asahara was something else, too—he was a man that people liked to believe. Other people were drawn to him, to his ideas, to his way of explaining them, to his personal presence. Asahara had a lot of charisma. With only his charisma, he built an international religion headquartered in Japan, with offices in the United States, Russia, and elsewhere. In only seven years, he had (according to some estimates) 50,000 followers.[2]

Different people have tried to explain the reason Asahara ordered the nerve gas attack, and there are many theories. Some say Asahara was angry at the Japanese government because he'd been arrested in 1982 for selling bogus medicine,[3] or because he'd been investigated for a real estate scheme in 1994.[4] Some say that he was trying to make one of his predictions come true: that there would be a world war involving nerve gas that would harm Japan.[5] Some say that he wanted to take over Japan and his failed attempt at getting himself and many of his followers elected to Japanese Parliament convinced him he had to do so by force.[6] Still others say that he was just angry at the world because he was mostly blind.[7]

But Japanese government lawyers prosecuting Asahara came up with another explanation, a theory that fits the events amazingly well with terrifying logic. The prosecutors explained that the attack was simply a means for Asahara to defeat a more powerful enemy, the Japanese police force.[8]

Police officers are part of a group that is called "emergency first responders"; the group also includes firefighters and emergency medical personnel. Those three sets of people are all the first ones called out to deal with an emergency. They have the training, experience, and equipment to deal with all sorts of crises and are modern society's defense against tragedy in almost every form.

Asahara hated and feared the Japanese police. He hated them because they represented a force that he could not defeat with his charisma, his money, or his followers; there were too many police, and they were well armed and well trained. He feared them for good

Personnel of the Self Defense Agency cleaning sarin off platforms after the 1995 terrorist attack on Tokyo's subways. *Getty Images*

reason: the government had been investigating Aum Shinrikyo for several years on many cases, including fraud, tax evasion, and even murder. The police would soon be knocking on the doors of the religion's offices, as well as Asahara's home; they had planned major raids of Aum facilities, to take place on March 22.[9] Asahara knew he had to fight or face prison and disgrace.

Aum Shinrikyo found itself in the same position as that of many small groups that want to fight larger, better-funded, better-armed groups: Aum needed a weapon that could defeat their enemies by killing or harming many of them without causing much damage to Aum.

Weapons of mass destruction offered the solution to that problem. The categories of weapons of mass destruction are sometimes called *NBCR*, which stands for Nuclear, Biological, Chemical, and Radioactive. Aum used sarin, which is a chemical nerve agent; Aum used it not only in the Tokyo subway attack, but also in an earlier attack on Matsumoto, a town north of Tokyo.[10] Aum used, or tried to use, other chemicals as well, such as VX, phosgene, and cyanide.[11] Aum also tried several smaller attacks using biological weapons like diseases, such as anthrax, Q fever, cholera, and botulism.[12] And there are reports claiming clear evidence that Aum tried to acquire nuclear weapons from Russia[13] and strains of the Ebola virus from Africa.[14]

NBCR weapons allow small, untrained groups to attack much larger, better-armed, better-equipped groups, using tactics and techniques that cause great damage to the large groups, but which pose much less threat to the smaller groups. These tactics are often called "asymmetric warfare," whether or not NBCR weapons are used. Aum was using asymmetric warfare to attack the Japanese government, particularly the police force.

Before the subway attack, the Japanese government had not been ignoring Aum. Many different law enforcement departments and organizations had been working, both together and separately, to investigate and prosecute Aum for various crimes. This included a great deal of counterterror efforts.

The police had been documenting earlier Aum attempts at using botulin toxin during the time frame of 1990-1995, and one attempt to deploy anthrax in 1993.[15] The government had also been investigating the group's involvement in several murders, including those of a prominent attorney and his family in 1989 and a notary public in 1995.[16] There had also been many complaints from the families of Aum members, suggesting that Aum was holding them against their will, forcing them to behave in a certain way, and would not let members leave the religion once they had joined. Several leaders of other religions and some journalists had also publicly criticized Aum; as a result, Aum assassins had targeted some of these critics.[17]

Police investigators had also gotten soil samples from the ground near Aum facilities suspected of producing NBCR weapons and had found trace evidence that sarin had once been present in those locations. Supposedly, the police also tried to send an undercover agent to join Aum, but the agent was killed in the attempt.[18]

Investigation and prosecution of Aum and Asahara were complicated by the group's status as a religion and the man's status as a religious leader. Japanese law, like the law in many modern societies, protects religious expression and practice, limiting government powers over religious groups and members. And Aum was both secretive and strict, allowing a small group of people inside the religion to conduct a lot of illegal activity, while the majority of members knew nothing (or little) about what was really going on.

Still, the Japanese law enforcement organizations functioned very well in their response; less than two months after the attack, raids had shut down a great many of the religion's business enterprises and spiritual centers, and 120 people had been arrested in connection with the sarin attack, including Asahara.

Asahara was found guilty of masterminding the March 20 attack and many legal charges associated with it. He was sentenced to death in 2004, after a trial lasting many years.

LESSONS LEARNED

While asymmetric warfare is commonly associated with terrorism, weapons of mass destruction—NBCR attacks—are, thankfully, fairly rare. The Aum Shinrikyo case taught both law enforcement personnel and other terrorists about aspects and problems associated with deploying weapons of mass destruction.

Government

- Outlandish and bizarre claims about the illegal and frightening practices of religious groups are not necessarily wrong or untrue; although it would have seemed unbelievable before the attack on the Tokyo subway, Aum actually was trying to get and use NBCR weapons.
- The long-term effects of a terrorist attack, or the activities of a terrorist group, can be devastating. In the years following the subway attack, the Japanese military learned that it had purchased a large amount of software products that had been designed by Aum computer engineers and that the products had secret "backdoors" built in, allowing Aum leaders to spy on the

Japanese military. Eradicating and replacing that software was extremely costly and time-consuming.

■ Governments of nation-states are very reluctant to use (and even test) weapons of mass destruction, but terrorists aren't. While the number of countries that have nuclear weapons continues to grow, only one nation has ever used them in an attack: that was the United States, and it happened more than 60 years ago. Fatal chemical weapons haven't been used in mass quantities since World War I; the Japanese allegedly used chemicals against China in the 1930s, and some rogue states have used them inside their own borders against minority groups, but governments don't commonly use deadly chemicals as a weapon. Terrorists, however, try to acquire NBCR weapons whenever they can, and are not afraid to deploy them (see Sidebar).

■ The public mail system can be an incredibly simple and destructive method for making attacks. Mail bombs and NBCR attacks have been perpetrated for decades, most notably by the Unabomber (See Chapter 9) and anthrax terrorists in the United States. Since 1996, the United States Postal Service has tried to reduce the likelihood and effectiveness of mail-borne attacks through a number of methods, such as creating a maximum weight on mail that can be dropped in anonymous USPS boxes and eliminating the practice of carrying mail on commercial passenger aircraft.[19]

Terrorists

■ Some NBCR weapons, especially chemical and biological ones, are very easy to get or make. The ingredients for them are often not illegal or expensive. But storing and deploying "weapons-grade" chemicals and biological agents (meaning, those that are the most deadly and "useful," in a military sense) is much, much more difficult. The sarin used in the Tokyo subway attack was *not* weapons-grade; had it been weapons-grade sarin, thousands, if not tens or hundreds of thousands of people would be dead, and many more permanently injured.

■ If a terrorist organization wants to conduct asymmetric warfare using NBCR weapons, having a lot of members in a terrorist group isn't nearly as important as having a good number of *educated* and *wealthy* members. Aum was particularly successful at recruiting many doctors, scientists, engineers, and other experts to work on their biochemical warfare projects, and people who had inherited a lot of money to finance their operations.

■ While it is useful for terrorist organizations to have members that are totally committed to the goals and way of life outlined by the terrorist leaders, it is even more useful to have members who are not easily recognized as being terrorists. Many of the Aum members at all levels of the organization had regular jobs and were, in many ways, just regular Japanese citizens. This provided Aum with a disguise for their more sinister plans and a group of people who could move about openly in Japanese society, gathering information and creating new sources of recruiting and financing.

■ Highly educated people of a different culture are more difficult to recruit than those among your own culture or less-educated people in other cultures. Aum was very successful in recruiting Japanese experts in elite fields such as medicine and science, and many other people with less education worldwide, but Aum was not at all successful in recruiting any Russian experts who were trained and experienced in creating and using NBCR weapons. Although Aum desperately wanted to use Russian scientists and weapons designers, none would join them.

COUNTERTERROR TACTICS

Even compared to terrorist methods that include bombs and automatic weapons, law enforcement personnel must be especially vigilant when it comes to possible NBCR attacks. The Aum Shinrikyo case can teach law enforcement personnel how to detect other potential perpetrators.

Effective

■ Following leads and assembling information from many different sources can help law enforcement and intelligence organizations combat terrorism, both before it occurs and afterward. Japanese police used a variety of sources, including news media, reports from citizens, and police patrol units, to assemble an overall notion of Aum's long-term warfare plans.

■ Science can be used to a great extent in detecting and combating high-tech threats. Soil samples extracted from the ground near Aum facilities showed trace compounds that result when sarin breaks down, which gave law enforcement clear evidence that Aum was working with chemical weapons.

■ Giving out as much public information about a threat as possible, without exaggerating, can help in preventing terror attacks. After the sarin subway attack, two other attacks using chemical weapons were stopped by alert citizens and public employees.[20] Keeping information secret from the public only makes the public a group of ignorant, helpless targets.

Ineffective

■ Trying to insert an undercover investigator into a group that uses sophisticated technology and research techniques, coupled with hypnotropic drugs and psychological techniques, is almost completely useless. Even worse, it is dangerous to the

⚲ SIMILAR NBCR TERROR ATTACKS

1984. Followers of the Bhagwan Sri Rajneesh spray *Salmonella* germs on food at a supermarket and the salad bars of 10 restaurants in Wasco County, Oregon. There are no fatalities, but 751 people are infected and 45 are hospitalized.[21]

2001. An estimated seven letters containing anthrax bacteria are mailed to various news media and political offices in the United States. Five people die, 12 are harmed, and thousands go on a strong course of antibiotics to prevent or treat infection. The crime has not been solved at the time of this publication.

2005. Four men use hydrogen cyanide gas to rob a card game in China; two of the robbers and all five card players die during the crime. The two surviving robbers are captured and sentenced to death in 2006.[22]

investigation and the investigator. An attempt by Japanese law enforcement to put an agent inside Aum almost surely led to that agent's death.

■ Making direct attempts to get inside information from current members of any religious group will often lead to failure, especially if they think the questioner will use the information against the group. Religious practitioners believe strongly in whatever religion they are involved with; even when faced with direct evidence that their religion has done something wrong, or makes no sense, the members of that religion will often stand by the religion and its leaders. Japanese law enforcement entities were much more successful in gathering information from former and current Aum members who approached the police first than those the police initiated contact with.

■ Trying to prosecute any group (for instance, a religion) in a jurisdiction where that group is protected by specific laws is very difficult.

The Future of Terrorism—The Future of Politics

On the morning of April 19, 1995, a rented truck was parked outside the Alfred P. Murrah Federal Building in Oklahoma City, Oklahoma. Inside the truck there was about 5,000 pounds of homemade explosives made from fertilizer and racing fuel. At 9:02 a.m., local time, the explosives were detonated and brought down half the building.

The explosion killed 168 people, 19 of them children.

An hour and a half later, Charles Hanger, an Oklahoma state trooper in Noble County, just north of Oklahoma City, pulled over Timothy McVeigh for driving a vehicle with no license plate.[1] As he approached the car, Hanger noticed that McVeigh was wearing a shoulder holster for a pistol and he arrested McVeigh on several misdemeanor charges related to carrying concealed weapons.

McVeigh was scheduled to be released on bail just two days later. Right before the Oklahoma authorities let him go, the FBI identified him as a likely suspect in the bombing of the federal building. The FBI had found a serial number on a piece of the rented truck, tracked the vehicle to the company that had rented it, and obtained information from the company employees, including a description of the renter and the phony contact information he had given.

McVeigh had undertaken the attack, the worst terrorist attack on American soil at that time, because he hated the federal government. He even cited specific events that turned him against the United States: these included situations at Ruby Ridge, Idaho, and

Investigators search the remains of the Alfred P. Murrah Building after it was bombed on April 19, 1995. *Greg Smith/Corbis*

Waco, Texas, where federal agents killed civilians.[2] McVeigh was later tried and convicted of several charges associated with the bombing and he was executed on June 11, 2001. A friend and co-conspirator, Terry Nichols, was sentenced to life in prison.

Like most terrorist attacks, the Oklahoma City bombing was resolved in the aftermath of a fatal, violent event. It put the government in a "reactive" stance, the position of reacting to terrorist actions. In such circumstances, the terrorists have the initiative: they choose when, how, and where to attack, and the government can only respond afterward.

If the conflict between terrorists and governments (or societies) is viewed as a war, which is how the terrorists often look at it, then the terrorists are in a much better position, both strategically (the big picture) and tactically (at the level of the actual fight). The decision of how, when, and where to fight can be a significant, if not key, element in the outcome of a battle or a war.

The terrorists have this advantage in any free nation or culture; in a free country, the government cannot arrest, prosecute, or use force against anyone until they have already done something wrong. Contrast this with totalitarian countries, where the governments can act against their own citizens for any reason, or no reason at all. When the totalitarian Soviet Union existed, there were not a lot of terrorist acts against it; once Russia became free, many terrorist groups started conducting attacks against that country.

Time is also on the side of the terrorist, especially if the terrorists' goals are revolution or overthrowing the government. Governments change, and those that exist in any form of democracy are comprised of politicians who constantly have to worry about re-election and are afraid of looking ineffective against terrorists. Governments are accountable to the citizens and are required to maintain annual budgets. Terrorist groups, on the other hand, can have the same leaders for years, spend their money all at once (or not at all), and do not answer to anyone because they're already criminals. The Irish revolutionary movement against the British can be said to have lasted over a hundred years, and the result was an independent Irish state. The same can be said for Zionist and Palestinian insurrections (approximately 50 years each). A terrorist outfit known as Euskadi Ta Azaktasuna (ETA), which means "Basque Homeland and Freedom," has championed the Basque

⚲ FUTURE TERROR TECHNIQUES: CYBERWARFARE

Can terrorists use computers? Just like every other political group, terrorist organizations use the Internet for communication, fundraising, and publicity. But can computers be used for actual acts of terrorism?

The definition of *terrorism* we used for this book includes the stipulation that "force" is used. If we say that *force* means "direct, physical harm," how can computers ever be said to be a use of force? Computers can cause physical harm; a virtual attack can lead to real-world damage. For instance, an angry Australian man used his own computer to hack into the computer network of a waste management organization in Queensland, Australia, and was able to make thousands of gallons of untreated sewage spill out onto streets, sidewalks, and yards. Hackers who can attack an air traffic control system, or even the street traffic lights at intersections, might do similar types of physical damage, and even more actual harm.

But if we think of *force* as meaning "measurable harm," then cyberterrorism is already under way in many parts of the world. Terrorists using computers have attacked entities, individuals, and even entire countries, trying to harm them *financially*. For instance, in April 2007 cyberattackers used thousands of "zombie" machines to attack the computer infrastructure of Estonia: they used "denial of service" attacks to shut down the Web sites and functionality of the Estonian president and prime minister, various government agencies, media outlets, schools, and banks.⁵ Experts suggest that the Russian government was in some way involved, and that mercenary computer hackers may have even been paid to conduct the attacks, which were most likely launched in retaliation for Estonia's removal of an old Russian statue. The damage and losses to the Estonian people are still being calculated, and some top officials are suggesting that this event—and others like it—are true threats to national security.

There is no doubt that terrorists can now include cyberattacks as one of their tools.

separatist movement in Spain. The ETA has killed more than 800 people in the past 30 years, but it has not yet succeeded in the political goal of creating a new Basque state in Spanish territory.[3]

As if that weren't bad enough, the government must rely heavily on law enforcement agencies to conduct counterterror activities, and law enforcement relies heavily on luck. McVeigh might not have been caught (or caught nearly as soon) if Trooper Hanger had not noticed the bulge of McVeigh's shoulder holster. Similarly, Eric Rudolph, who exploded a bomb at the 1996 Summer Olympics in Atlanta, Georgia, and several other bombs at abortion clinics and a nightclub, was captured many years later by a regular patrol cop on his beat, and not by specially trained or equipped counterterror forces.[4] And Ted Kaczynski, known as "the Unabomber," conducted a deadly terror campaign over *20 years* and was only finally caught when his own brother turned him in to authorities.

Governments are also hindered by their structure. Governments have to follow the law, and have to follow the processes that ensure they are just and legal. For instance, governments often take a lot longer than terrorists to use new technologies; government agencies (especially the military) must go through specific procedural steps before adopting a new technology, especially if that technology will be used near the government's own citizens or in the government's own territory. Terrorists, of course, don't have such restrictions: terrorists are often the first-adopters (the group that uses a new technology when it first comes out) of combat technology, and can therefore avoid detection or capture, because the government does not yet know how to counter the new technology.

Another dangerous aspect in the fight against terror is the constant risk that the government might make a mistake or overstep its power, and thus cause further harm. This can even be true of situations that don't involve terrorists at all. For instance, on February 28, 1993, when federal troops tried to serve an arrest and search warrant and storm a Branch Davidian religious compound in Waco, Texas, in order to seize illegally modified firearms, a battle ensued. It eventually developed into a 51-day siege that culminated in a final federal attempt to subdue the occupants of the compound with a form of tear gas. In response, the Branch Davidians began to set fires that grew out of control and left 76 of the religion's members dead (including 21 children).[6] Similarly, in August 1992, when federal agents tried to arrest Randy Weaver at his home in Ruby

Visitors to the Oklahoma City National Memorial walk among empty chairs that signify those lost in the Oklahoma City bombing. *David Butow/Corbis SABA*

Ridge, Idaho, for selling illegally modified weapons several years before, a gunfight erupted, which resulted in the death of a federal agent and an 11-day siege, and ultimately led to federal snipers killing a 14-year-old boy and his 42-year-old mother while she was holding a baby in her arms.[7] Also, while acting irresponsibly in the wake of the Olympic bombing in 1996, federal agents illegally told news media sources that Richard Jewell, a security guard at Centennial Park when the bomb was detonated, was a prime suspect in the case; Jewell was later totally exonerated, and, indeed, lauded as a hero.[8]

Therefore, governments fighting against terrorism run the risk of accidentally or purposefully resorting to terror tactics. But governments continually attempt to modify counterterror tactics to make them more effective. According to Jerry R. DeMaio, a trial attorney with the United States Justice Department's Counterterrorism Section from 2002 to 2006, the government is trying to become less reactive and more pre-emptive. "Until 9/11, terrorism crimes were often investigated the same way—after the terrorist act," explains DeMaio. "But because the potential for death and destruction is so high with crimes of terrorism, law enforcement agencies like the FBI are now focused on preventing attacks, not just reacting after a terrorist attack happens."[9]

DeMaio goes on to explain that, "Because the focus of law enforcement has changed, the crimes that terrorists are charged with have also changed. Instead of facing trial for murder, kidnapping, hijacking, or using explosives, would-be terrorists now often face charges of supporting terrorism. 'Supporting' usually means giving money, goods, weapons, or even oneself to a terrorist group, to help carry out that group's intentions."

In this way, government operatives hope to prevent terror attacks before they happen, as opposed to punishing terrorists after an attack has occurred.

This might become even more difficult in the future. If recent history is any indication, terrorism is actually increasing in direct proportion to counterterror efforts; that is, the more money, personnel, and legislation governments task to fight terrorists, the more terrorism takes place.[10]

There are many possible reasons this is true. It could be that more private groups and citizens are collecting power that was once only held by governments; these nongovernmental entities can fund and take part in wars (especially guerilla or terror wars, which are far cheaper than conventional wars), which are the types of actions only governments could have conducted previously. Examples of such groups include al Qaeda, the revolutionary army FARC in Colombia, and any person or group that can acquire NBCR weaponry.

Or maybe even governments have realized that conventional wars (that is, wars betweens armies) are too expensive, both in terms of money and in people, as well as international prestige, so

(continues on page 112)

⚲ WEAPONS AND TACTICS USED IN ARMED COUNTERTERROR OPERATIONS

Stun (or "Flash-bang") grenades. These devices were specifically designed for the British SAS for use in counterterror
operations. They were first deployed in Operation Magic
Fire, the storming of Lufthansa Flight 181 (see Sidebar,
Chapter 7), when the SAS provided them to the German
GSG9 counterterror forces. The stun grenade emits an
incredibly bright burst of light (the "flash"), at the same
time as a very, very loud noise (the "bang"), which disori-
ents and confuses the targets (usually terrorists confined
inside a small space, such as the cabin of an airliner or an
apartment). Counterterror forces can then enter that area
and dispatch targets with little to no resistance.

Silenced weapons. Sometimes during counterterror operations,
surprise is a significant element in deciding the outcome.
Sneaking up on and eliminating terrorists without alerting
other terrorists can be a major concern. In this case, loud
weaponry such as firearms and grenades don't really help.
Therefore, many counterterror forces have adopted the
use of guns with suppressors (also known as "silencers").
Some of these weapons are manufactured specifically for
use by special forces personnel in counterterror situations,
with the suppressors built right into the gun, such as the
Heckler and Koch MP5SD3.

Three-round burst/"Double-tap." In the mid-twentieth century, firing rates of firearms increased dramatically; guns
could throw more bullets in less time than ever before.
Strangely enough, however, there didn't seem to be a
matching increase in the number of people killed or inca-
pacitated per bullet. The main reason for this was the lack
of accuracy that occurs in a rapid-fire weapon after the
third trigger pull. As more bullets are launched, the accuracy of the weapon decreases. Because of this, many elite
military forces adopted the "double-tap" technique (see
"Lessons Learned," Chapter 4), where the trigger is pulled
quickly, twice in a row, then the shooter pauses, and then

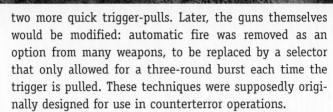

two more quick trigger-pulls. Later, the guns themselves would be modified: automatic fire was removed as an option from many weapons, to be replaced by a selector that only allowed for a three-round burst each time the trigger is pulled. These techniques were supposedly originally designed for use in counterterror operations.

Sophisticated surveillance equipment. Being able to look at, hear, or otherwise detect the positions, numbers, and disposition of the terrorists themselves is very important in planning military attacks on terrorist targets. That is why many counterterror military forces utilize state-of-the-art electronic detection gear years before it is used commonly in consumer goods. For instance, fiber optic cameras were used to pierce and observe the interior of the Iranian embassy in London in 1980 (see Sidebar, Chapter 6) so the British SAS could identify the number and location of the terrorists inside.

A soldier fires an AK-47 style assault rifle equipped with a silencer. Silencers are commonly used to maintain the element of surprise in counterterror operations. *Leif Skoogfors/Corbis*

(continued from page 109)

they have opted instead to use terrorists as their military employees, or terror activity as their battlefield tactics. This might be said for Iran, which is purported to supply weapons, training, and funding to terrorist groups such as Hezbollah.

Another theory is that the more counterterror activity governments conduct, especially militaristic, pre-emptive counterterror activity, the more terrorists are created, supported, or motivated. When governments use force against someone, that person, and people that know that person, tend to resent the government; some of them may want to "fight back" against that government, or just lend support to someone who will. McVeigh, for instance, was said to have been taking revenge for the federal attacks on the religious compound in Waco, Texas, and the Weaver family at Ruby Ridge; the Oklahoma City bombing took place two years to the day after the federal attack in Waco.

Terrorism is not new; it has existed since one human first tried to frighten another into doing something. While terrorism may be on the rise, it is not inevitable or unstoppable. Governments are constantly formulating new ways to conduct counterterror operations and to prevent terrorism. Many guerilla campaigns and terrorist groups have failed and disintegrated in the past; it is possible to triumph over terror.

September 11, 2001, and the War on Terrorism

The events of September 11, 2001, are perhaps the most widely known example of modern terrorism. Because of their recency and magnitude, though, it is impossible, right now, to explain the effects of those events in historical terms. Therefore this chapter is unlike any of the others in this book. It will explore some of what is known about that day and what has happened since, but it is not intended to be a definitive analysis of 9/11.

In New York City on September 11, 2001, the day started with a bright morning and clear skies. Rush hour traffic filled the streets and subways as people went through their morning routines on their way to work. But at 8:46 a.m. the first sign that something terrible was occurring that day rippled through the city. At that moment, American Airlines Flight 11, flying out of Logan International Airport in Boston with 92 people onboard, slammed into the north tower of the World Trade Center, a skyscraper in lower Manhattan. Emergency services responded quickly, but before anyone fully understood what was taking a place, a second plane, United Airlines Flight 175, also out of Logan International Airport in Boston and with 56 people aboard, struck the second World Trade Center tower at 9:03 a.m.

The worst terrorist attack ever conducted on United States soil was underway.

This series of photographs shows hijacked United Airlines Flight 175 as it approaches (upper left) and impacts the World Trade Center's south tower (upper middle). A gaping hole can be seen in the north tower (right) as a result of a similar attack minutes earlier. *Sean Adair/Reuters/Corbis*

Live television coverage of the first crash started almost immediately, and people around the nation were watching when the second impact occurred, making it clear that the collisions had not been accidents. But the attack was not over yet.

At 9:37 a.m. American Airlines Flight 77, out of Washington Dulles Airport and with 59 people onboard, crashed into the western face of the Pentagon. Security cameras recorded the impact.

Less than half an hour later, at around 9:59 a.m., the south tower of the World Trade Center, which had sustained major structural damage from the impact and resulting fire, collapsed. At 10:03 a.m. a fourth plane, United Airlines Flight 93 out of Newark Liberty International Airport and with 44 people onboard, went down in a field near Shanksville, Pennsylvania. It's believed United 93's intended target was the White House or the U.S. Capitol in Washington, D.C.

At 10:28 the north World Trade Center tower fell.

♀ DECEPTIONS UNDETECTED

In the process of planning and carrying out the 9/11 attacks, the terrorist hijackers committed numerous lesser crimes. Many of them, as foreign citizens, should not have been in the United States, but remained due to irregularities that went overlooked or ignored. The 9/11 Commission determined that opportunities existed "for intelligence and law enforcement to exploit al Qaeda's travel vulnerabilities. Considered collectively, the 9/11 hijackers

- included known al Qaeda operatives who could have been put under constant law enforcement surveillance;
- presented passports manipulated in a fraudulent manner;
- presented passports with suspicious indicators of extremism;
- made detectable false statements on visa applications;
- made false statements to border officials to gain entry into the United States; and
- violated immigration laws while in the United States."[1]

Today, in an effort to combat terrorism, the government is adding a counterterror element to almost all government agencies, including those involved with immigration and customs. This might someday allow government law enforcement operatives to halt a terrorist attack before it occurs. It may also force those people and entities that conduct criminal activity (like those that smuggle people into the United States and falsify paperwork) to become even better at what they do. It is an odd reality of counterterrorism that the more aggressive a government is in trying to fight terror, the more places terrorists find to hide.

By this time all flights in the United States had been cancelled and all airplanes, other than military planes, had been grounded to prevent another attack. The United States was on high alert, and a new chapter in American history had begun.

Fatalities from the attacks numbered 2,974. All people onboard the four planes perished, as did 125 on the ground at the Pentagon and 2,603 who were in the World Trade Center at the time of impact or when the towers collapsed. As of this writing, 24 people remain missing, lost that day at the World Trade Center.

FBI investigators excavate the crash site of United 93 in Shanksville, Pennsylvania. It is likely that the terrorists aboard the plane intended to crash it into the White House or the Capitol. *Gene J. Puskar/AP*

As investigators put the pieces together, a shocking picture emerged. Organized terrorist cells had hijacked each of the fatal flights that morning. The terrorists seized control of the planes, probably by threatening the crew and passengers with weapons or bombs, real or fake. Then they directed the planes toward predetermined targets with fatal precision, except for United 93.

Five hijackers took over each of the other flights, but there were only four on United 93. Also, as word spread of the initial attacks, passengers in contact with friends and family via cell phones knew that the United States was under attack and that their plane was about to become a deadly missile. Making a brave decision, the passengers challenged the hijackers and prevented them from redirecting United 93 toward its target.

The hijackers were soon linked to a group of Islamic terrorist organizations called al Qaeda, which means "the Base" in Arabic.

The horrifying actions of the September 11 attacks soon became known simply as "9/11," for the month and day on which they took place. According to *The 9/11 Commission Report*, the 9/11 attacks were not the first time al Qaeda had tried to destroy American property and hurt or kill Americans. A group with links to al Qaeda had attacked the World Trade Center in 1993 with a truck bomb, killing six people and wounding a thousand more. In 1995 police in the Philippines discovered plans by Ramzi Yousef, a man connected to al Qaeda, to blow up a dozen American airplanes while they flew over the Pacific Ocean. Between 1993 and 2001 the United States experienced numerous attacks sponsored or supported by al Qaeda, including:

- a 1995 car bomb in Riyadh, Saudi Arabia, which killed five Americans and two others
- coordinated truck bombings at U.S. embassies in Nairobi, Kenya, and Dar es Salaam, Tanzania, resulting in 224 deaths, including 12 Americans, and thousands wounded
- a foiled plot to bomb Los Angeles International Airport in December 1999, a failed attempt to sink U.S. Navy ship the USS *The Sullivans*, and a plan to target several Jordanian locations where American tourists gathered, all part of the so-called Millennium Plot

- an al Qaeda attack on the USS *Cole* in a port in Aden, Yemen, which killed 17 American sailors and nearly sunk the ship[2]

Al Qaeda states that it is angry with the United States of America for many reasons. Some Muslims find American military bases in Saudi Arabia offensive because Saudi Arabia is a holy land for Islam, and most Americans are not Muslim. They also dislike American support of the nation of Israel, which many Muslims see as an evil, illegitimate country. They resent American popular culture and its popularity around the world because many devout Muslims find it distasteful, ugly, and obscene. Also, one of al Qaeda's most senior leaders, a wealthy Saudi named Osama bin Laden, helped the mujahadeen, Afghan freedom fighters, expel Soviet military forces that invaded Afghanistan in 1979. The mujahadeen had support and training from the United States. They felt betrayed when the United States abandoned Afghanistan at the same time the Soviets withdrew, despite American promises to help rebuild the country and heal the wounds caused by the war.

In response to the 9/11 attacks, the United States government launched a Global War on Terror with the goal of tracking many terrorists and terrorist organizations around the world, smashing their resources, and bringing them to justice. Immediate actions included freezing financial assets of several known terrorists, such as Osama bin Laden, and pursuing terrorists linked to the 9/11 attacks who were hiding in Afghanistan and Pakistan. After Afghanistan's government, the Taliban, refused to cooperate, the United States and its allies invaded Afghanistan. They toppled the Taliban government and killed or captured many terrorists. Some escaped to the mountainous region of the border between Afghanistan and Pakistan, where Osama bin Laden is believed to be hiding today.

The Global War on Terror has since expanded to include increased information sharing among the intelligence agencies of different nations, more aggressive surveillance of known and suspected terrorists, and greater efforts to interrupt terrorist sources of financing.

LESSONS LEARNED

The National Commission on the Terrorist Attacks Upon the United States, also called the 9/11 Commission, found: "The 9/11 attacks were a shock, but they should not have come as a surprise. Islamist extremists had given plenty of warning that they meant to kill Americans indiscriminately and in large numbers."[3]

Government

- Inadequate analysis and assessment of information within intelligence and law enforcement organizations, such as the Central Intelligence Agency (CIA) and the Federal Bureau of Investigation (FBI) prevented optimum cooperation. The FBI, for example, did not have the ability to connect information between its field agents that might have uncovered the terrorist plot; at the time, many FBI agents did not even have personal Internet connections in their workplace.
- Limitations on how the CIA could deal with terrorists abroad led to lost opportunities to capture or kill Osama bin Laden before 2001. In particular, relying on proxies, or local allies and informants, in places like Afghanistan, rather than acting directly, frustrated CIA efforts to combat al Qaeda.
- Bureaucratic difficulties kept different law enforcement and spy groups from sharing information with each other. For instance, the CIA is only supposed to act outside the borders of America so that it does not spy on American citizens, even by accident. The CIA, the FBI, the Defense Security Services (DSS), the National Security Agency (NSA), and many other groups did not work well together because each wanted to be the one agency that is the most important, or best, at conducting counterterror operations.

Terrorists

- To carry out the 9/11 attacks, the terrorists exploited lax security in the United States. Several of the 9/11 hijackers were in the country illegally with fraudulent visas and passports. Additionally, airport security personnel failed to detect the simple, but deadly, box cutters the hijackers smuggled onto the airplanes. Without the resources to mount a direct, armed attack against the United States, the terrorists identified and exploited key weak spots. Any free nation will always have vulnerabilities, and any smart, determined enemy can find them.

- A large country with a large government and a large military will always be reactive. This means that the people assigned to protect the country will always focus on the previous attack against that country, while the terrorists can concentrate on the *next* attack. The terrorists, in that way, have an upper hand. They can come up with new ways to attack that the government hasn't even considered yet.

COUNTERTERROR TACTICS

Effective

- Freezing their money makes it more difficult for terrorists to carry out their plans. Funding for terrorist groups come from many sources. Wealthy extremists like Osama bin Laden finance terror, but so do sympathetic individuals who make personal donations. Cooperation among governments has helped to identify and lock the bank accounts used by terrorists. In the United States efforts have been launched to investigate several organizations claiming to be charities but which may actually be funneling money to terror groups.
- Changing public opinion and regular procedures about how to respond to imminent or ongoing attack. Before 9/11, members of the public, crew members of American airlines, and even military personnel, were instructed to cooperate at all times with armed kidnappers and hijackers because cooperating was the most likely way to survive a hostage situation. On 9/11 the terrorists involved took advantage of this to crash three out of the four jets they had captured. On the fourth jet, the passengers and crew decided they would rather die than be used as weapons, and prevented the plane from reaching its target. In several situations after 9/11, passengers have participated in defending aircraft from crazed, disturbed, or violent people on board and subduing the troublemakers.

Ineffective

- Trying to keep pace with each and every potential risk against American targets is impossible. For example, after Richard Reid, a British al Qaeda sympathizer, tried to use bombs hidden in his shoes to blow up a plane on the way to the United States, all passengers were required to remove their shoes for inspection before boarding planes at American airports. After a plot involving liquid and gelatin explosives was detected in England, travelers were banned from having more than three ounces of liquids or gels on board a plane. Terrorists will always come up with new and clever ways of conducting attacks. Trying to prevent each one of those attacks becomes more and more expensive, frustrating, and time-consuming. There is no evidence to suggest anyone is safer because passengers have to remove their shoes and throw away their water bottles before getting onto a plane, but the procedures continue.

- In response to fears that American air travel was vulnerable to hijacking, the federal government created the Transportation Security Administration (TSA). Under TSA, all airport security personnel, including those who work at the X-ray machines and metal detectors, became employees of the federal government. The theory was that federal employees would make airports more secure. About four years later, several factors led the government to believe just the opposite, and new guidelines were put in place to encourage use of private security companies at airports. Private companies, for instance, can hire people faster, and can fire them, if needed, while government employees are much more difficult to discipline.[3]

These are just a few of the lessons that have emerged since 9/11. There will no doubt be many, many more to come.

Chronology

1850–1880s The Irish Republican Brotherhood (IRB) tries to overthrow the British government presence in Ireland, mainly using a terrorist campaign.

1859 Abolitionist John Brown captures the armory at Harpers Ferry, West Virginia, as a protest against slavery. He is captured and executed.

1865 Several men in the southern United States form the Ku Klux Klan (KKK), first as a cultural response to the northern victory during the Civil War, then as a terrorist organization meant to oppress blacks and other minorities.

1867 Dynamite, a stable form of the explosive nitro-glycerine, is patented by engineer Alfred Nobel. It would be used as a terrorist tool almost immediately.

1879–1890s The Narodnaya Volya use terrorist tactics against the Czar of Russia and his government. They kill the czar, but fail in fomenting ultimate revolution.

1880s The telephone is introduced in the United States, and almost immediately used by criminals for nefarious purposes, including terrorism. Soon thereafter, monitoring and recording telephone calls ("wiretapping") became a tool used by governments to counter criminal activity.

1903 The Wright brothers make the first powered airplane. With air travel possible, international combat, including terrorism, becomes much easier.

1903–1906 The governments of Russia and some Baltic and Eastern European states sponsor attacks, known as "pogroms," against Jews living in their territories.

1910–1922 The IRB is resurrected as a political body, and takes part in more guerilla warfare. The group is disbanded in 1922, in accordance with a treaty agreement.

1914 Archduke Franz Ferdinand of Austria is assassinated by separatist terrorists who want to form their own country of Serbia/Yugoslavia.

1915 Turkish forces massacre Armenians in a terrorist policy to dominate Armenian territory.

1922–1969 The Irish Republican Army (IRA) is assembled from disenfranchised members of the defunct IRB and other nationalist groups. The IRA wages what may possibly be the longest sustained guerilla campaign of the twentieth century, carrying out many tragic terrorist acts, including assassinations, bombings, and murders.

1927–1949 Mao Zedong leads the Red Army in using guerilla and other revolutionary tactics to overthrow the Chinese government and form a new communist Chinese nation.

1929–1948 Zionist groups use terrorism (among other tactics) to secure the area of British-occupied Palestine and form a new modern nation, Israel. These groups include the Irgun, the Haganah, The Stern Gang, and Lehi.

1941–1956 Politician Ho Chi Minh forms the Viet Minh to use insurgent tactics to overthrow French imperial claims, and create a new modern state of Vietnam and resist Japanese occupation during World War II. In 1956 the Viet Minh is dissolved after the Allies cede North Vietnam to nationalist forces.

1945 The United States tests the first atomic bomb. With the invention of nuclear weapons, a new opportunity for terror arises. From this date onward, much effort will be expended trying to keep atomic weapons away from terrorists.

1946–1954 The Huks, a nationalist guerilla group, try to overthrow the new government of the post-World War II Philippines, which is installed by and sympathetic to the Allied powers. The movement fails, and the Huks are disbanded.

1950–1972 The Pathet Lao conduct an armed insurrection to dominate Laos and are eventually successful.

1953–1959 The 26 of July Movement, led by Fidel Castro, conducts a terrorist insurrection to overthrow the president of Cuba. They are eventually successful.

1950s–present The submachine gun, a compact firearm with automatic-fire capability, becomes a popular weapon of choice among both terrorists and counterterrorism forces.

1959–present In Spain a group called the ETA begins a decades-long terrorist campaign to create a new modern Basque nation by taking land from Spain.

1960–1976 The Viet Cong (VC) is a terrorist organization that conducts guerilla warfare against the South Vietnamese government and their American sponsors. The Vietnamese Army absorbs the VC when the country is reunified after the Vietnam War in 1976.

1961–1992 The Umkhonto we Sizwe fight racist apartheid policies in South Africa, and are eventually successful; the government is overthrown, and a new constitution drafted, in 1992.

1964–present The Palestine Liberation Organization (PLO) conduct a guerilla campaign to overthrow the state of Israel and create a new modern country, Palestine. They become known for several dramatic, infamous acts of terrorism.

1965–1970s The Black Panthers conduct many terrorist, anti-government activities, in the hopes of eventually attaining equality for blacks. The group disintegrates in the 1970s.

1967–1976 The peak period for airplane hijackings, during which hundreds occur.

1969–1977 The Weather Underground Organization conducts a series of shootings, bombings, and other paramilitary activity in protest of American government policies such as the Vietnam War and discrimination against minority groups. The group starts to disband in 1977, and most members eventually turn themselves in to authorities.

1969–present The Provisional Irish Republican Army (PIRA) resumes the guerilla campaign against British occupation of Ireland after the fractionalization of the IRA. The armed insurgency continues until 2005, when the PIRA agrees to end armed attacks in return for political concessions from the British, and becomes a political group.

1972 The PLO stages a massive attack on the Israeli team at the Olympic games in Munich, Germany. Eventually, they kill 11 athletes and a German police officer before security forces kill all the terrorists.

1978–1985 The MOVE organization in Philadelphia conducts an anti-government campaign, at one point killing a police officer and wounding several others. The group is crippled in 1985, when the local police drop a bomb on the roof of their rowhouse, burning it and 61 other homes, killing 11 people, five of them children.

1978–1996 Dr. Theodore John Kaczynski, known as "the Unabomber," conducts a mail bomb campaign in the United States, mainly because he disliked aspects of modern American society. His bombs kill three and injure 23 more. He is captured in 1996, and eventually sentenced to life in prison.

1979–1992 The mujahadeen in Afghanistan conduct a guerilla war against Soviet invaders, using many terrorist tactics. The mujahadeen are trained and equipped by the United States. Eventually, the Soviets are beaten and leave Afghanistan.

1980s The personal computer becomes affordable and popular, changing the face of modern communications.

1980–1992 The Sendero Luminoso, or "Shining Path," a Communist terrorist organization funded by drug money, attempts to take over Peru. After years of atrocities committed by both the terrorists and the government, the Shining Path is ruined when its leader is captured in 1992.

1983 Two terrorists drive trucks filled with explosives into the U.S. Marine barracks in Beirut, Lebanon, killing 241 Americans, 58 French personnel, and six civilians. The courts would later conclude that the attackers were part of Hezbollah, sponsored by Iran.

1994 A civil war between the Hutus and the Tutsis in Burundi leads to genocide, with some 800,000 people massacred. Armed forces use murder and rape as terrorist tactics to conquer their opposition.

1995 Timothy McVeigh and Terry Nichols plan and execute a truck bomb attack against the federal building in Oklahoma City, Oklahoma, killing 168. McVeigh is eventually executed, and Nichols is sentenced to life in prison.

1995 Members of the Aum Shinrikyo religion deploy sarin nerve gas in the Tokyo subway system, killing 12 people and harming about a thousand more. All the attackers are captured, and the religion's leader is arrested.

2001 On September 11, 19 hijackers crash two jetliners into the World Trade Center, one into the Pentagon, and one in a field in Pennsylvania, killing nearly 3,000 people.

2002 Terrorist bombs in Bali, Indonesia, a popular tourist destination, kill 202 people and injure 209 in the worst terrorist attack in Indonesian history. Members of terrorist group Jemaah Islamiya are convicted of the attack in 2003.

2004 A terrorist cell inspired by al Qaeda bombs a commuter train in Madrid, Spain, on March 11, killing 191 and wounding 1,755 in a successful effort to sway Spain's general elections held three days later.

2005 Four suicide bombs blast through London, England's public transportation system on the morning of July 7, leaving 52 victims dead and 700 injured in the worst terrorist attack in London's history.

2006 Police in the United Kingdom uncover and prevent a terrorist plot to detonate liquid explosives onboard a number of aircraft while in flight between the U.K. and destinations in the United States and Canada.

2007 Two car bombs are discovered and disarmed before-detonating in London on June 29. The next day terrorists attack Glasgow International Airport in Scotland, attempting to drive a car bomb into the airport, but security barriers prevent the vehicle from entering the terminal.

Endnotes

Chapter 1

1. Desmond Ryan, *The Fenian Chief: A Biography of James Stephens* (Coral Gables, Fla.: University of Miami Press, 1967), 256.
2. Terry Golway, *For the Cause of Liberty: A Thousand Years of Ireland's Heroes* (New York: Simon and Schuster, 2000), 9.
3. Richard English, *Armed Struggle: The History of the IRA* (Oxford: Oxford University Press, 2003), 8.
4. London Metropolitan Police Web site. http://www.met.police.uk/so/special_branch.htm. Accessed on August 9, 2006.
5. Ryan, *The Fenian Chief: A Biography of James Stephens*, 316
6. Leon O'Broin, *Revolutionary Underground: The Story of the Irish Republican Brotherhood, 1858–1924* (Totowa, N.J.: Rowman and Littlefield, 1976), Preface.

Chapter 2

1. Vera Broido, *Apostles Into Terrorists* (New York: Viking Press, 1977), 193.
2. Ibid., 193.
3. Adam Ulam, *In The Name of the People* (New York: Viking Press, 1977), 338.

4. Margaret Maxwell, *Narodniki Women* (New York: Pergamon Press, 1990), 54.
5. Broido, *Apostles Into Terrorists*, 181.

Chapter 3

1. Yehuda Lapidot, "The Raid on the Jerusalem Officers' Club," Etzel, the Irgun Web site. http://www.etzel.org.il/english/index2.html. Accessed on September 9, 2006.
2. J. Bell, *Terror Out Of Zion* (New York: St. Martin's Press, 1977), 190.
3. Kati Marton, *A Death In Jerusalem* (New York: Pantheon Books, 1994), 107.
4. Bell, *Terror Out Of Zion*, 190.
5. Ibid.
6. Ibid.

Chapter 4

1. Blair House Web site. http://www.blairhouse.org/e_tru assassin-p.html. Accessed on September 27, 2007.
2. Stephen Hunter, and John Bainbridge, Jr., *American Gunfight: The Plot To Kill Harry Truman - And The Shoot-Out That Stopped It* (New York: Simon & Schuster, 2005), 293.
3. Ibid., 266.
4. Ibid., 317–319.

5. Manuel Roig-Franzi, "A Terrorist In The House." Washingtonpost.com. http://www.washingtonpost.com/ac2/wp-dyn/A48918-2004Feb17. Updated on February 22, 2004.

6. Robert Guzman. "Filiberto Ojeda: Hero or Terrorist?" Puertorican.com Web site. http://puertorican.com/prcom_guzman306_905d.html. Accessed on June 12, 2007.

7. *New York Times.* "8 Military Jets Destroyed At Air Base in Puerto Rico." January 12, 1981. http://query.nytimes.com/gst/fullpage.html?res=9F04E0D6173BF931A25752C0A967948260&n=Top%2fNews%2fU%2eS%2e%2fU%2eS%2e%20States%2c%20Territories%20and%20Possessions%2fPuerto%20Rico. Accessed on September 26, 2007.

8. Office of the Inspector General. "A Review of the September 2005 Shooting Incident Involving the Federal Bureau of Investigation and Filiberto Ojeda Ríos." United States Department of Justice. http://www.usdoj.gov/oig/special/s0608/chapter2.htm. Updated on August 2006.

9. Federal Bureau of Investigation press release. "FBI Responds to OIG Report on the Circumstances Surrounding the Attempted Capture of Filiberto Ojeda." Federal Bureau of Investigation. http://www.fbi.gov/pressrel/pressrel06/oigreport080906.htm. Updated August 09, 2006.

Chapter 5

1. Laura Heath, "An Analysis of the Systematic Security Weaknesses of the U.S. Navy Fleet Broadcast System, 1967–1974, as Exploited by CWO John Walker." Federation of American Scientists. http://www.fas.org/irp/eprint/heath.pdf, pages 61–72. Accessed on June 17, 2007.

2. Gaddis Smith, Book review of Robert Liston's, *The Pueblo Surrender.* (New York: M. Evans and Co., 1988), on the Web site of *Foreign Affairs*, Spring, 1989. http://www.foreignaffairs.org/19890301fabook7434/robert-a-liston/the-pueblo-surrender.html. Accessed on December 27, 2007.

3. Ed Brandt, *The Last Voyage of the U.S.S. Pueblo* (New York: W.W. Norton and Company, Inc., 1969), 175.

Chapter 6

1. "Operation Red Hat." Global Security. http://www.globalsecurity.org/military/ops/achille_lauro.htm. Accessed on December 27, 2007.

2. BBC News. http://news.bbc.co.uk/onthisday/hi/dates/stories/october/7/newsid_2518000/2518697.stm. Accessed September 27, 2007.

3. Carl Rochelle, "After Nearly 11 Years, EgyptAir Hijacker Sentenced." CNN. http://www.cnn.com/US/9610/07/terrorst.sentenced/index.html. Accessed on December 27, 2007.

Chapter 7

1. Steven Emerson and Brian Duffy, *The Fall of Pan Am 103: Inside the Lockerbie Investigation* (New York: G.P. Putnam's Sons, 1990), 98.
2. "Consular information page on Libya," U.S. State Department Web site. http://travel.state.gov/travel/cis_pa_tw/cis/cis_951.html. Accessed on December 27, 2007.

Chapter 8

1. Centers for Disease Control and Prevention. "Facts About Sarin." http://www.bt.cdc.gov/agent/sarin/basics/facts.asp. Accessed on June 27, 2007.
2. J. Poolos, *The Nerve Gas Attack on the Tokyo Subway* (New York: The Rosen Publishing Group, 2003), 15.
3. Ibid., 11.
4. The Centers for Disease Control and Prevention. http://www.cdc.gov/ncidod/EID/vol5no4/olson.htm. Accessed on December 27, 2007.
5. Mark Jurgensmeyer, *Terror In The Mind of God: The Global Rise of Religious Violence* (Berkeley: University of California Press, 2000), 109–111.
6. Centers for Disease Control and Prevention, op. cit.
7. Poolos, 15.
8. Centers for Disease Control and Prevention, op. cit.
9. Robert Lifton, *Destroying the World to Save It: Aum Shinrikyo, Apocolyptic Violence, and the New Global Terrorism* (New York: Henry Holt and Company, 1999), 39.
10. Ibid., 6.
11. Ibid., 40–41.
12. Centers for Disease Control and Prevention, op.cit.
13. Lifton, 6.
14. Centers for Disease Control and Prevention, op.cit.
15. Centers for Disease Control and Prevention, op.cit.
16. Poolos, 9–10.
17. Lifton, 40.
18. Ibid., 40.
19. Bob Anderson, United States Postal Service spokesperson. Interview by the author, June 28 and August 4, 2006.
20. The Federation of American Scientists Web site. http://www.fas.org/irp/congress/1995_rpt/aum/index.html. Accessed on December 27, 2007.
21. The *Detroit News* Web site. http://www.detnews.com/apps/pbcs.dll/article?AID=/20061124/LIFESTYLE03/611240348. Accessed on February 11, 2007.
22. People's Daily Online. http://english.people.com.cn/200609/20/eng20060920_304643.html. Accessed on December 4, 2006.

Chapter 9

1. *Indianapolis Star*. "The Oklahoma City Bombing." IndyStar.com. http://www2.indystar.com/library/factfiles/crime/national/1995/oklahoma_city_bombing/ok.html. Accessed on January 21, 2007.

2. CNN. "McVeigh: Gulf War Killings Led Him On The Path To Disillusionment." http://archives.cnn.com/2000/US/03/13/mcveigh/. Last updated on March 13, 2000.

3. BBC News. "Who Are ETA?" http://news.bbc.co.uk/1/hi/world/europe/3500728.stm. Accessed on January 21, 2007.

4. CBS News. "Olympic Bomber: 'I Apologize.'" http://www.cbsnews.com/stories/2005/08/22/national/main789086.shtml. Accessed on January 21, 2007.

5. Steven Myers, "Cyberattack on Estonia Stirs Fear of 'Virtual War.'" International Herald Tribune. http://www.iht.com/articles/2007/05/18/news/estonia.php. Updated on May 18, 2007.

6. PBS. "Waco: The Inside Story." http://www.pbs.org/wgbh/pages/frontline/waco/. Accessed on January 21, 2007.

7. David Lohr, "Randy Weaver: Siege at Ruby Ridge." Court TV Crime Library. http://www.crimelibrary.com/gangsters_outlaws/cops_others/randy_weaver/15.html. Accessed on January 21, 2007.

8. Media Libel, "Richard Jewell V. NBC, and Other Richard Jewell Cases." http://medialibel.org/cases-conflicts/tv/jewell.html. Accessed on January 21, 2007.

9. Jerry DeMaio, former United States Deputy Attorney. E-mail interview by the author, December 12, 2006.

10. Susan Glasser, "U.S. Figures Show Sharp Global Rise In Terrorism." Washington Post. http://www.washingtonpost.com/wpdyn/content/article/2005/04/26/AR2005042601623.html. Updated on April 27, 2005.

Chapter 10

1. The National Commission on the Terrorist Attacks Upon the United States. "The 9/11 Commission Report: Executive Summary." http://govinfo.library.unt.edu/911/report/911Report_Exec.htm. Accessed February 5, 2008.

2. The National Commission on the Terrorist Attacks Upon the United States. "The 9/11 Commission Report." http://govinfo.library.unt.edu/911/report/911Report.pdf. Accessed February 5, 2008.

3. The National Commission on the Terrorist Attacks Upon the United States, op. cit.

4. Thomas Frank, "Lawmakers to Encourage Private Airport Screeners." USA Today. http://www.usatoday.com/news/nation/2005-10-04-screeners_x.htm. Accessed March 17, 2008.

Bibliography

Air University Library Publications. "Terrorist and Insurgent Organizations." Available online. URL: http://www.au.af.mil/au/aul/bibs/tergps/tgaum.htm (accessed on June 29, 2007).

Bartlett, Thomas, and Keith Jeffrey, eds. *A Military History of Ireland*. Cambridge: Cambridge University Press, 1996.

BBC/H2G2. "A Hijack on the High Seas." Available online. URL: http://www.bbc.co.uk/dna/h2g2/A730900 (accessed on June 29, 2007).

BBC News. "1985: Gunmen Hijack Italian Cruise Liner." Available online. URL: http://news.bbc.co.uk/onthisday/hi/dates/stories/october/7/newsid_2518000/2518697.stm (accessed on June 29, 2007).

Bell, J. Bowyer. *Terror Out Of Zion: Irgun Zvai Leumi, LEHI, and the Palestine*. New York: St. Martin's Press, 1977.

Bew, Paul. *Land and the National Question in Ireland, 1858–82*. Atlantic Highlands, N.J.: Humanities Press, Inc., 1979.

Bilgili, Ata. "M.S. Achille Lauro," Dartmouth University Student Web page. Available online. URL: http://engineering.dartmouth.edu/~Ata_Bilgili/Ships/ITALIAN/STARLAURO/ACHILLE_LAURO/achillelauro.htm (accessed on June 29, 2007).

Blair House. "Events: Truman Assassination Attempt." Available online. URL: http://www.blairhouse.org/e_truassassin-p.html (accessed on June 29, 2007).

Brandt, Ed. *The Last Voyage of the U.S.S. Pueblo*. New York: W.W. Norton and Company, Inc., 1969.

Broido, Vera. *Apostles Into Terrorists*. New York: Viking Press, 1977.

CBS News. "Olympic Bomber: 'I Apologize.'" CBS Broadcasting, Inc. Available online. URL: http://www.cbsnews.com/stories/2005/08/22/national/main789086.shtml (accessed on January 21, 2007).

Central Intelligence Agency. "Puerto Rico," The World Fact Book. Available online. URL: https://www.cia.gov/library/publications/the-world-factbook/geos/rq.html (accessed on November 20, 2007).

Chaliand, Gerard, ed. *Guerilla Strategies: An Historical Anthology from the Long March to Afghanistan*. Berkeley: University of California Press, 1982.

Cohen, Susan, and Daniel Cohen. *Pan Am 103: The Bombing, the Betrayals and a Bereaved Family's Search for Justice.* New York: Penguin Books, 2000.

U.S. Department of State. "Consular Information Sheet: Libya." Available online. URL: http://travel.state.gov/travel/cis_pa_tw/cis/cis_951.html (accessed on June 29, 2007).

Cordesman, Anthony. *Terrorism, Asymmetric Warfare, and Weapons of Mass Destruction: Defending the U.S. Homeland.* Westport, Conn.: Praeger Publishers, 2001.

Cronin, Isaac, ed. *Confronting Fear: A History of Terrorism.* New York: Thunder's Mouth Press, 2002.

Detroit News. Available online. URL: http://www.detnews.com/apps/pbcs.dll/article?AID=/20061124/LIFESTYLE03/611240348 (accessed on February 11, 2007).

Dunnigan, James F., and Austin Bay. *A Quick and Dirty Guide To War: Briefings on Present and Potential Wars,* 3d ed. New York: William Morrow and Company, 1996.

Emerson, Steven, and Brian Duffy. *The Fall of Pan Am 103: Inside the Lockerbie Investigation.* New York: Penguin Group, 1990.

English, Richard. *Armed Struggle: The History of the IRA.* Oxford: Oxford University Press, 2003.

Global Security. "Achille Lauro." Available online. URL: http://www.globalsecurity.org/military/ops/achille_lauro.htm (accessed on June 29, 2007).

Golway, Terry. *For the Cause of Liberty: A Thousand Years of Ireland's Heroes.* New York: Simon and Schuster, 2000.

Hanle, Donald. *Terrorism: The Newest Face of Warfare.* McLean, Va.: Pergamon-Brassey's, 1989.

Harry S. Truman Library and Museum. Available online. URL: http://www.trumanlibrary.org/ (accessed on June 29, 2007).

Heath, Major Laura. "An Analysis of the Systematic Security Weaknesses of the U.S. Navy Fleet Broadcast System, 1967–1974, as Exploited by CWO John Walker," Federation of American Scientists. Available online. URL: http://www.fas.org/irp/eprint/heath.pdf (accessed on June 29, 2007).

Heller, Joseph. *The Stern Gang: Ideology, Politics, and Terror, 1940–1949.* London: Frank Cass, 1995.

Herzog, Chaim. *The Arab-Israeli Wars: War and Peace in the Middle East from the War of Independence through Lebanon.* New York: Random House, 1984.

Hunter, Stephen, and John Bainbridge Jr. *American Gunfight: The Plot To Kill Harry Truman—and the Shoot-out That Stopped It.* New York: Simon & Schuster, 2007.

IndyStar.com. "The Oklahoma City Bombing." *Indianapolis Star*. Available online. URL: http://www2.indystar.com/library/factfiles/crime/national/1995/oklahoma_city_bombing/ok.html (accessed on January 21, 2007).

Jeffreys-Jones, Rhodri. *The CIA and American Democracy*, 3d ed. New Haven: Yale University Press, 2003.

Jewett, Robert, and John Lawrence. *Captain America and the Crusade Against Evil: The Dilemma of Zealous Nationalism*. Grand Rapids, Mich.: William B. Eerdmans, 2003.

Jurgensmeyer, Mark. *Terror In The Mind of God: The Global Rise of Religious Violence*. Berkeley: University of California Press, 2000.

Khouri, Fred. *The Arab Israeli Dilemma*. Syracuse, New York: Syracuse University Press, 1985.

Lampert, E. *Sons Against Fathers: Studies in Russian Radicalism and Revolution*. London: Oxford University Press, 1965.

Lapidot, Yehuda. "The Raid on the Jerusalem Officers' Club." Available online. URL: http://www.etzel.org.il/english/index2.html (accessed on September 9, 2006).

Lifton, Robert. *Destroying the World to Save It: Aum Shinrikyo, Apocalyptic Violence, and the New Global Terrorism*. New York: Henry Holt and Company, 1999.

Liston, Robert. *The Pueblo Surrender*. New York: M. Evans & Company, 1991.

Lohr, David. "Randy Weaver: Siege at Ruby Ridge." Court TV Crime Library. Available online. URL: http://www.crimelibrary.com/gangsters_outlaws/cops_others/randy_weaver/15.html (accessed on January 21, 2007).

Long, David. *The Anatomy of Terrorism*. New York: Free Person, 1990.

Marton, Kati. *A Death In Jerusalem*. New York: Pantheon Books, 1994.

Maxwell, Margaret. *Narodniki Women: Russian Women Who Sacrificed Themselves for Freedom*. New York: Pergamon Press, 1990.

Media Libel. "Richard Jewell v. NBC, and other Richard Jewell Cases." Available online. URL: http://medialibel.org/cases-conflicts/tv/jewell.html (accessed on January 21, 2007).

Metropolitan Police. "Special Branch." London Metropolitan Police. Available online. URL: http://www.met.police.uk/so/special_branch.htm (accessed on August 9, 2006).

Myers, Steven Lee. "Cyberattack on Estonia Stirs Fear of 'Virtual War.'" *International Herald Tribune*. Available online. URL: http://www.iht.com/articles/2007/05/18/news/estonia.php.

The National Park Service. "Blair House." Available online. URL: http://www.cr.nps.gov/nr/travel/wash/dc25.htm (accessed on November 20, 2007).

O'Broin, Leon. *Revolutionary Underground: The Story of the Irish Republican Brotherhood, 1858–1924.* Totowa, N.J.: Rowman and Littlefield, 1976.

The Official Site of the USS Pueblo Veterans' Association. Available online. URL: http://www.usspueblo.org/ (accessed on June 29, 2007).

Olson, Kyle B. "Aum Shinrikyo: Once and Future Threat?" Centers for Disease Control and Prevention. Available online. URL: http://www.cdc.gov/ncidod/EID/vol5no4/olson.htm (accessed on June 29, 2007).

Pape, Robert. *Dying To Win: The Strategic Logic of Suicide Terrorism.* New York: Random House, 2005.

PBS. "Waco: The Inside Story." Available online. URL: http://www.pbs.org/wgbh/pages/frontline/waco/ (accessed on January 21, 2007).

People's Daily Online. "Two Men Executed for Killing Seven with Poison Gas in Robbery." Available online. URL: http://english.people.com.cn/200609/20/eng20060920_304643.html (accessed on December 4, 2006).

Poolos, J. *The Nerve Gas Attack on the Tokyo Subway.* New York: The Rosen Publishing Group, 2003.

Rogger, Hans. *Russia in the Age of Modernisation and Revolution, 1881–1917.* New York: Longman Publishing Group, 1983.

Ryan, Desmond. *The Fenian Chief: A Biography of James Stephens.* Coral Gables, Fla.: University of Miami Press, 1967.

Senate Government Affairs Permanent Subcommittee on Investigations. "Global Proliferation of Weapons of Mass Destruction: A Case Study on the Aum Shinrikyo." Federation of American Scientists. Available online. URL: http://www.fas.org/irp/congress/1995_rpt/aum/index.html (accessed on June 29, 2007).

"The Smashing of the Van," CSU-Fresno. Available online. URL: http://www.csufresno.edu/folklore/ballads/Pga050.html (accessed on August 5, 2006).

Stern, Jessica. *The Ultimate Terrorists.* Cambridge: Harvard University Press, 2001.

Ulam, Adam. *In The Name of the People: Prophets and Conspirators in Prerevolutionary Russia.* New York: Viking Press, 1977.

United States Navy's Naval Vessel Register. "USS Pueblo (AGER 2)" Available online. URL: http://www.nvr.navy.mil/nv rships/details/AGER2.htm (accessed on June 29, 2007).

United States Secret Service. "How Protection Works." U.S. Secret Service. Available online. URL: http://www.secretservice.gov/ protection_works.shtml (accessed on June 29, 2007).

The Washington Post Online. Available online. URL: http://www. washingtonpost.com/wpsrv/inatl/longterm/panam10/timeline. htm (accessed on December 10, 2006).

Further Resources

Books

Begin, Menachem. *The Revolt*. New York: Dell Books, 1978.

Bethel, Elizabeth. *The Palestine Triangle*. Putnam Publishing Group, 1979.

Clarke, Thurston. *By Blood and Fire*. London: Hutchinson & Company, 1981.

Cohen, Aharon. *Israel and the Arab World*. New York: Funk and Wagnalls, 1970.

Liston, Robert A. *The Pueblo Surrender: A Covert Action by the National Security Agency*. New York: M. Evans & Company, 1988.

Web sites

Associated Press. "Six School Terrorists 'from Chechnya,'" *Sydney Morning Herald*.
http://www.smh.com.au/articles/2004/09/10/1094530816831.html

Chivers, CJ. "The School," *Esquire*.
http://www.esquire.com/features/articles/2006/060610_mfe_June_06_School_1.html

Storobin, David. "The Rise and Fall of Chechen Independence Movement," *Global Politician*.
http://www.globalpolitician.com/articleshow.asp?ID=990&cid=4&sid=35

Sydney Morning Herald. "Six School Terrorists 'from Chechnya.'"
http://www.smh.com.au/articles/2004/09/10/1094530816831.html

Ortega, Sergio. "This Is a Hijack!" AirOdyssey.net.
http://www.airodyssey.net/articles/hijack.html

Zionism and Israel Information Center. "Haganah—A History of the Underground Jewish Defense Force in Israel."
http://www.zionism-Israel.com/Haganah.htm

Index

Page numbers in *italics* indicate images.

About the Author

Ben Malisow holds a degree in military history from the United States Air Force Academy. While in the military, he was trained by the U.S. Army in small-unit tactics and tools, received Department of Defense certification as an interrogator for the SERE (Survival, Evasion, Resistance, and Escape) School, and took part in covert counternarcotics operations in the Southern Hemisphere. His writing has appeared in various publications, such as ANSER's *Homeland Defense Journal*, SecurityFocus.com, and the SANS Reading Room, among others. Malisow has an MBA and teaches English at the College of Southern Nevada.

About the Consulting Editor

John L. French is a 26-year veteran of the Baltimore City Police Crime Laboratory. He is currently a crime laboratory supervisor. His responsibilities include responding to crime scenes, overseeing the preservation and collection of evidence, and training crime scene technicians. He has been actively involved in writing the operating procedures and technical manual for his unit and has conducted training in numerous areas of crime scene investigation. In addition to his crime scene work, Mr. French is also a published author, specializing in crime fiction. His short stories have appeared in *Alfred Hitchcock's Mystery Magazine* and numerous anthologies.